Nostalgic
TEESSIDE

The publishers would like to thank the following companies for their

support in the production of this book

Main sponsor
K Home International

Atha and Co

AV Dawson Ltd

R C Ayres

The Cleveland Centre

Fawcett & Hetherington

Harrison Packaging

INEOS Nitriles

Middlesbrough College

C.L. Prosser

QA Weld Tech Ltd

Geoffrey Robinson Ltd

Sahaviriya Steel Industries

A Suggitt Ltd

Svitzer Marine

Teesside University

William Lane Ltd

First published in Great Britain by True North Books Limited
England HX3 6SN
01422 244555
www.truenorthbooks.com

ISBN 978 - 1906649876

Text, design and origination by True North Books

Nostalgic
TEESSIDE

CONTENTS

INTRODUCTION

Such has been the popularity of our previous books on the Teesside area, that we have been encouraged to produce a new publication. Our books allow readers to walk on cobbled streets, browse in well known local shops of the period and revisit special events and occasions, without leaving the comfort of their favourite armchair.

The title of this new book, 'Nostalgic Teesside', tells you all you need to know about what is captured within its pages. Turning over leaf after leaf will bring you to a treasure trove from the last century. Through the photographs and thoughtful text, the reader is taken on a ride back through the mists of time to an age when mum would nip into Woolworths and dad could buy a suit at the Fifty Shilling Tailor.

We make no apologies for the fact that some of the photographs will be outside living memory because they will still be familiar to us. They may feature an event described to us by a close relative or they could feature historical landmarks such as bridges and buildings.

Whatever the view taken on the boundaries which separate 'history', 'nostalgia' or 'the present', we should all invest a little time occasionally to reflect on the past and the people and events which helped to shape life as we know it today.

The companies and organisations that have thrived in the area, over the recent decades, are many. The Teesside Urban Area has a proud tradition of creativity, enterprise and innovation and we take great pleasure in including in this book, histories of an outstanding selection of different companies, whose contribution to the development and sustainability of the city's economic prosperity is a matter of record. With their co-operation and access to their respective photographic archives, we have been able to tell their stories. Hopefully, this will trigger the memories of local people who have worked for them, or been touched by their part in community life.

Teesside has always been vibrant and buzzing with energy, but different episodes in its life can be seen here. So, think of youthful days at the old dance hall or courting in the cinemas of old and be entertained again as we revive Nostalgic Teesside…Happy memories!

TEXT	STEVE AINSWORTH, ANDREW MITCHELL, TONY LAX
PHOTOGRAPH RESEARCH	TONY LAX
DESIGNER	SEAMUS MOLLOY
BUSINESS DEVELOPMENT MANAGER	PETER PREST

ON THE TEES

The Transporter Bridge is one of only about 20 of its type ever built. About half that number are still in existence, but this is the longest of those and measures 851 feet in length. Although it was out of use for a couple of years in the late 1990s following some structural and operational problems, it has been functioning for over 100 years, providing an unusual sight for visitors as they head along Riverside Park Road or into town from the direction of Stockton-on-Tees. Although the Tees provided a means of access both to the sea and out to the west, it was a natural north-south barrier that required the creation of crossing points. A ferry, using rowing boats, was in place in the early 19th century and a steamer service was inaugurated in 1862. But more was needed to meet the demands of industry and local inhabitants going about their daily routines. Ten years on and Charles Smith, manager of a Hartlepool ironworks, came up with the idea of an 'ariel ferry'. However, this was not acted upon and larger steamships were built instead. It was not until 1906 that the debate about a transporter bridge was resurrected. In the following years, Parliament agreed the Bill authorising the construction of such an iconic means of crossing the river. Arrol's, a Glaswegian firm, won the contract, costed initially at just over £68,000. Seen in this group of pictures during its construction, inauguration and early operation, the bridge was completed at about 25 per cent over budget.

The opening ceremony was performed by Prince Arthur of Connaught on 17 October, 1911, officiating on a specially built viewing platform. It takes but two minutes to cross to or from Port Clarence and there is a regular service on the quarter hour for much of the day.

Teesside's first blast furnace was built in 1851 after the discovery of iron ore in the Cleveland Hills. New railway lines were being built across the country which was contributing to the massive growth in demand of iron. More and more blast furnaces were opened in the vicinity of Middlesbrough to meet this demand, and by the end of the century Teesside was producing about a third of the nation's iron output. In 1875, Bolckow and Vaughan opened the first Bessemer Steel plant in Middlesbrough. With the development of methods to use local iron ores, the Tees was destined to become 'the Steel River'. Taken from high up on the Transporter Bridge, this 1926 view of the Tees and the riverside industries shows a relatively tranquil and smoke free day, which is very surprising considering the amount of working chimneys there was back then. Normally, chimneys belched out their fumes and workers and residents alike had to exist in that polluted atmosphere. It is little wonder that chest complaints and respiratory problems abounded. But our grandparents had to endure all this in order to make a living. Times were hard during those inter-war years. The country never recovered properly from the recession brought on by the vast financial outlay demanded of our nation's coffers in the Great War. During the 1920s, Britain was hit by the General Strike and this photograph could be linked to the strike which lasted nine days, from 4 May to 13 May 1926.

This is a rare view from some 180 feet above the River Tees, during the construction of the Newport Bridge. The bridge spans the River Tees a short distance upriver from the Transporter Bridge, linking Middlesbrough with the borough of Stockton-on-Tees. What a fabulous view these workmen have as they stand on top of one of the twin lifting towers constructed to support the bridge. Built by local company Dorman Long, it was said to be the heaviest of its type in the world, and was officially opened to traffic on 28 February, 1934, by Prince Albert, the Duke of York. Originally twelve men were needed to man the bridge around the clock, as during the 1940s and 1950s it had to be raised up to twice a day. The lifting span is now sealed as the number of ships needing to sail up to Stockton-on-Tees declined. The legal requirement to lift the bridge for shipping traffic was removed in 1989 after the repeal of a Parliamentary Act, although to this day the Tees Newport Bridge still serves as a road bridge. In recognition of its rarity and uniqueness in being a building of special architectural and historical interest, the bridge was given Grade II Listed Building status in 1988.

1855, a huge force of 50,000 troops, jointly commanded by Lord Raglan and General Canrobert, besieged and finally captured the city. The gun was a trophy acquired by the council in 1857. Too large to fit on a mantelpiece in the Town Hall, it was sited near St Hilda's Church. In later years it was moved to a prominent position in Albert Park, before going on its travels once more, arriving in Stewart Park c1950. On 21 May, 1965, the Territorials took it under their wing, moving the gun to their headquarters on Stockton Road.

Above: Looking east along the river, this scene dates from c1900. The view includes ships on the stocks at the Craig Taylor shipyard. This was a seven-acre site, functional from 1884 to 1930. Its first boat was the Saint André, a cargo vessel that foundered near Boulogne in 1908. The Portregis was the last to roll down the slipway. It became a war casualty in 1940 when torpedoed by a U-boat. During the second half of the 19th century, the new technology associated with iron shipbuilding and its related industries was to be a major cause of Stockton becoming an important manufacturing centre. The vessels on the Stockton side of the river in the picture are a mix of steam and wind powered craft.

Right: A manoeuvre which needed council workmen and Territorial Army personnel to join forces. The gun was a relic of the Battle of Sebastopol, one of the epic events of the Crimean War. This important naval base was vital to the Russian Black Sea fleet in the war against Britain and France. From 17 October, 1854, to 11 September,

This fabulous photograph gives a true prospective on the immense size of the massive Athel Line tankers. Crew members look tiny as they peer over the prow of the Athelsultan, during the launch at Smith's Dock in 1951. It must have been an unforgettable moment from this select band of invited guests and well-wishers, as they cheer and wave as the ship eventually gathers forward momentum and slips graciously into the water for the first time. Shipbuilding at Smith's Dock had been going on in the Northeast since 1907.

AROUND THE STREETS

Below and right: Manfield was a long established seller of boots and shoes, dating back to 1844. It occupied a prime site on the corner of Newport Road and Linthorpe Road and, as can be seen from the number of shoppers there in c1900, did a roaring trade. The Wesley Central Mission, over the way, first opened its doors to a congregation on Sunday, 20 September, 1863. It was a grand building, with room for 800 to be seated and listen to the sermons delivered to them. A day school was established in 1865 and a splendid organ installed in 1899. The slightly later image from the Edwardian era also shows Linthorpe Road, with the now demolished Co-operative Society buildings on the left. Further down, the tower of St George's Congregational Church can be seen. Its first services were held in 1894. It was damaged by enemy action in the summer of 1942, but was repaired and continued to serve its parishioners until 1966. The prominent building on the right is the Grand Opera House. It was built at the junction with Southfield Road on land known as Satters Catt. Fairs and an agricultural show had been formerly held there. The Grand Opera House opened in 1903, but was converted to a cinema in 1931. It closed in 1964.

Below: Heading southwest away from the town centre, Middlesbrough's Newport Road takes us towards the roundabout and junction with the A66 and the Tees Bridge Approach Road. It was a much quieter scene in the early years of the last century. The buildings we see here have all gone, with the likes of Aldi and KwikFit now to be seen on the left. The quirky St Paul's Church, opposite Cannon Park Way, was once a noticeable feature. Designed by Austin and Johnson, its foundation stone was laid by Mrs Hustler of Acklam Hall on 25 June 1870. Consecrated a year later on 14 December, it served its parish until 1966 and was demolished 12 months further down the line.

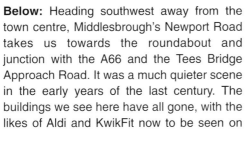

The public transport revolution took Britain by storm, in the last few years of Queen Victoria's reign, when horse drawn trams were replaced on the road by electric trams. Electric cabling began to criss-cross our towns, and Stockton got its first taste of this on Monday 16 July, 1898. Stockton had an advantage over many of its contemporaries, in as much as the High Street was a broad highway that could cope with twin tram tracks. They were laid along the eastern side of the street, leaving plenty of room on the opposite side, where carters and stallholders could operate without fear of being run down. We can see this clearly in this fantastic photograph, as two trams, No 30 and 46, pass the Cash Clothing Company at the end of the 19th Century.

There were many such spots as Constable's Yard to be found on the east side of Middlesbrough, down near the Riverside Tavern. Here was a damp, dank and dingy part of town where eking out an existence in 1925 was a difficult and well nigh impossible task. They may have escaped the workhouse, but life offered little joy for these women. Nostalgic nonsense such as 'We were poor but we were happy' is just that – nonsense.

Above: A washing line strung along Jackson's Terrace, Jubilee Road, with an old fashioned hand cranked mangle in front, suggests this might have been a Monday. That was, for many, the traditional wash day. Pictured in the first quarter of the last century, this block of housing was home to families thrown together as a community that would help one another get by. Adult neighbours were known as 'Auntie' and 'Uncle' to the children. Everyone pulled together against the common enemy – poverty.

Above: This road runs for several miles from Yarm and is seen here just a few hundred yards short of Stockton town centre. The small tree on the right is now many feet higher, but the stripes on the triangular gables of the houses seem not to have altered. The view was captured looking from within reach of the Queen Victoria Girls' School, now replaced by a pub. St Peter's Church is just out of shot on St Peter's Road, to the right, but St Cuthbert's on Spring Street, further to the left, was yet to be built. The religious building we can see is that of the Methodist Church. It was officially opened on 29 September, 1904 by Mrs J Wilson Watson.

Happily, this picture of children playing on a Victorian terrace street in Middlebrough gives no indication of the devastation caused throughout the country during the Second World War. By the end of the war over 200 buildings had been destroyed within the Middlesbrough area. Things would never be the same again, as areas of early and mid-Victorian housing were demolished and much of central Middlesbrough was redeveloped. Heavy industry was relocated to areas of land better suited to the needs of modern technology. Middlesbrough itself began to take on a completely different look. This picture is unidentified, but it could well be part of the Cannon Street area of Middlesbrough where strong community values prevailed. The housing consisted of a large number of cheaply built terrace streets, mainly to accommodate the iron and steel works workers. While the menfolk were out at work, mum was at home doing the daily chores. Standards had to be maintained and women would spend ages scrubbing their front step and even scrubbing the pavement outside their house until it was spotless. One of the children in photograph has a brush in hand, but I am not sure how much sweeping she intends to do.

Below: Dovecot Street was once a bright and lively part of Stockton's shopping scene, but it is now rather cut off from the main centre and, in truth, parts of it look quite run down these days. It is unlikely ever to regain its level of importance as the shops along High Street now dominate the area. Wellington Square and Castlegate centres also supply the sort of competition that is well nigh impossible to counter.

Below: By 1944, petrol rationing was so keen that only short, essential journeys were permitted. Stockton's Church Row, by now called Church Road, would normally have had many motor cars moving

along past the old police station, but it would be another couple of years before the family motor was wheeled back out of its mothballed state. This photograph was probably taken from a window of the then Robinson's store (now Debenhams) opposite the Parish Church and The Castle & Anchor. The area of Church Road past the old Police Station has seen many changes since this picture was taken, with the building of the swimming baths and municipal buildings. The concrete structures in front of the main building may well have been required as some sort of bomb blast protection as Stockton was the target of Nazi bombers on several occasions during the war.

Below: At one time there was a bell inside the Town House tower that was rung to warn of a fire. That was all rather primitive, if reasonably effective, but a far cry from the efficient response seen here from over 60 years ago as firemen got to grips with a blaze in a three-storey chemical warehouse on Bridge Road. In the early 19th century, those who had their property insured with Norwich Union were entitled to the services of a fire engine. It was not until much later that a proper service, available to all, was established. Stockton Fire Station No 1 opened in 1883 on West Row/Prince Regent Street. It remained in use until 1965, but was not demolished until over 30 years later.

A long line of 1960s parked cars and the Parish Church dominate this excellent photograph of Stockton High Street. Many changes have been made along this street over the years including pedestrianisation, however, the overall structure remains largely unchanged. This elevated view taken from the Town House shows the north end of the one of the widest High Street's in England on a busy non market day. The Parish Church of St Thomas, or more commonly simply Stockton Parish Church, was built in 1712 and stands on the east side of the High Street, with the white columns of the War Memorial in front. The tall building on the opposite side of the street is thought to be the earliest surviving steel framed building in the UK - 'Robinson's Coliseum' department store which opened in 1901 and is now owned by Debenhams. The articulated lorry pulling out of Bishop Street on the right would not be able to do so today as the road is blocked off and a bus shelter is situated on the pavement.

popular place of entertainment. Next to the ABC, further away from the camera in this picture, the modern building housing W. Duncan's Supermarket can be seen just past Middle Street. In the block housing Maxwell's School Outfitters, which gave the corner its name, Sam's Friendly Furnishers and the G-Plan centre can also be seen.

Below: A preserved Middlesbrough Corporation Guy Arab IV/Northern Counties, registration EXG 892, seen here approaching the mini roundabout in front of Saltburn Railway Station in April 1974. The image is more interesting when you consider this is a place where it would never have appeared when it was in service. Saltburn station was designed by the Architect William Peachey and completed in 1862. Passenger services had begun in August 1861 but a start on the permanent building was delayed while the directors finalised their ideas for the Zetland Hotel. In its heyday, the station had four platforms and a sizeable number of carriage sidings to handle the large quantities of excursion trains that ran there - these included services from Leeds and Blackpool. The railway-owned Zetland Hotel was opened at the rear of the station in 1863 and this meant passengers in first class carriages could disembark directly into their accommodation. Around the time of this photograph, a remodelling scheme saw the station reduced in size, with the two main platforms and signal box being taken out of use.

Above: A delightful view looking towards Maxwell's Corner, taken in the late 1950s or early 1960s. The Castle and Anchor, a Vaux public house, can be seen in the foreground on the right at the end of Church Road. The impressive ABC 'Globe' stands at No. 90 High Street, it can be seen here showing the feature 'Who's Minding the Store?' starring Jerry Lewis and the lovely Jill St. John. Sadly, the building no longer serves as a cinema and is offered for the sale at the time of writing. For a time after 1978 the building served as a bingo hall, but even this was not commercially successful enough to preserve its role as a

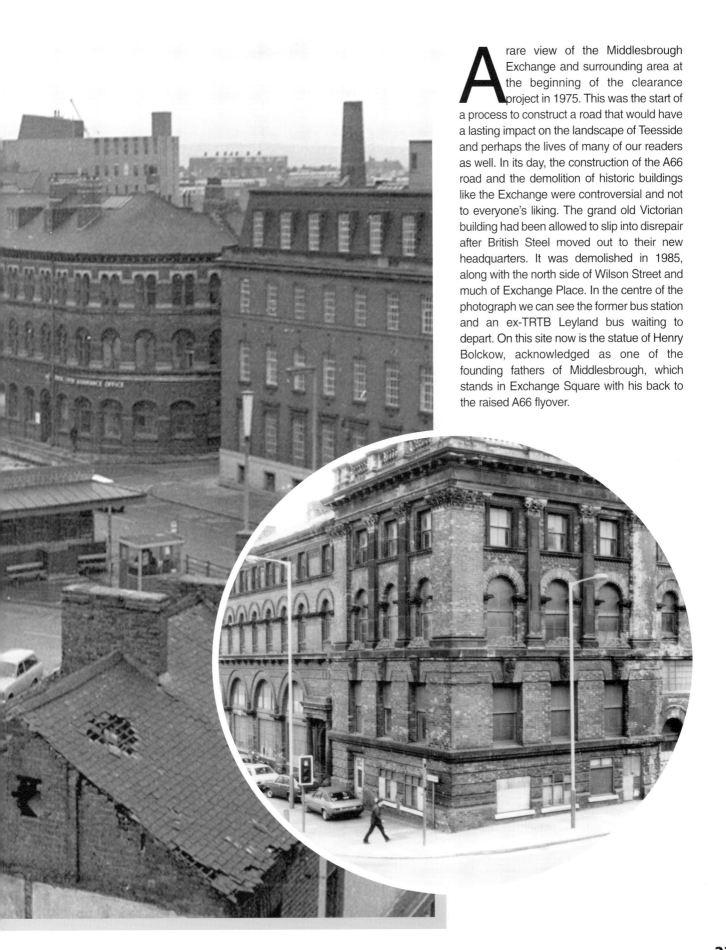

A rare view of the Middlesbrough Exchange and surrounding area at the beginning of the clearance project in 1975. This was the start of a process to construct a road that would have a lasting impact on the landscape of Teesside and perhaps the lives of many of our readers as well. In its day, the construction of the A66 road and the demolition of historic buildings like the Exchange were controversial and not to everyone's liking. The grand old Victorian building had been allowed to slip into disrepair after British Steel moved out to their new headquarters. It was demolished in 1985, along with the north side of Wilson Street and much of Exchange Place. In the centre of the photograph we can see the former bus station and an ex-TRTB Leyland bus waiting to depart. On this site now is the statue of Henry Bolckow, acknowledged as one of the founding fathers of Middlesbrough, which stands in Exchange Square with his back to the raised A66 flyover.

It is only when you look at the traffic on a still photograph from the second half of the last century that we realise that major congestion on our roads has a long history. The motor car became a necessity for every family once the Swinging 60s got under way. Yet, within a couple of decades it had come to dominate and strangle our town centres. It was not long before Redcar joined the ranks of those towns that restricted parts of their thoroughfares and turned part of High Street into a pedestrian-only shopping district. Some of the businesses have gone, but the likes of the Marks & Spencer name continues to thrive. But, nothing lasts forever; just ask Woolworths and Comet.

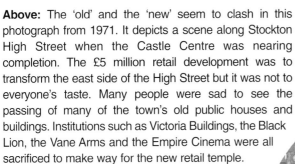

Above: The 'old' and the 'new' seem to clash in this photograph from 1971. It depicts a scene along Stockton High Street when the Castle Centre was nearing completion. The £5 million retail development was to transform the east side of the High Street but it was not to everyone's taste. Many people were sad to see the passing of many of the town's old public houses and buildings. Institutions such as Victoria Buildings, the Black Lion, the Vane Arms and the Empire Cinema were all sacrificed to make way for the new retail temple.

Right Here we can see the very recognisable façade of the British Home Stores building, which dominates this picture from 23 July, 1969. The Town Hall clock tower is on the top left of the picture and a variety of 1960s cars add interest to the scene. To the right is the site of the former Manfield Store which was demolished to make way for Binns Department Store, now renamed as House of Fraser. The location is, of course, the busy corner of the Newport, Linthorpe and Corporation Roads. Before the British Home Stores building was constructed part of the site was

occupied by the imposing brick-built Wesley Chapel (see page 7), which had stood on the spot since 1863. Demolition came in the mid-1950s and the congregation relocated to Park Wesley Chapel.

This is a really interesting elevated view looking out across the docks area of Middlesbrough, probably from the late 1970s. The dominant feature in the foreground is the Dragonara Hotel on Fry Street, which opened in 1972 and today is recognisable as the 130 bedroom Thistle Hotel. There are many different makes of car are lined up along Gurney Street, which meets at the junction with Corporation Road, in the bottom right of this shot. Over to the left, we can make out the protruding figure of the Dock Clock Tower, built around 1870. It supplied water for

accumulators and reservoirs for maintaining water pressure to dockside cranes and dock gates. It also became useful as a navigation mark on the River Tees and is only a stones throw away from the Transporter Bridge. The A66 dual carriageway runs across from left to right of this picture and development work looks to be taking place at the time. What is interesting is that if we took the photograph today we would clearly see the home of Middlesbrough Football Club in the top right of shot. Opened in 1995, the North Stand of the Riverside Stadium backs on to the River Tees at this point.

ON THE HOME FRONT

Above: On 31st August 1939, just four days before the formal declaration of war was made, Operation Pied Piper was put into action. Over the next few days, some 3,000,000 people were evacuated from the towns and cities marked down by the government as being at threat from enemy action. Most were children and long lines of them formed orderly queues at bus and railway stations. Carrying small, battered suitcases, along with ubiquitous gas masks, they had identification tags around their necks and made a heart rending sight as they left their parents and made their way to strange destinations in villages and more rural settings. The trauma of separation for these young evacuees, most of whom did not fully understand what was going on, stayed with many of them for years. Some had pleasant experiences, being welcomed into new homes with open arms. Others, though, were regarded as pests and intruders and made to feel unwanted. Some billets were quite out of the ordinary. A group of children from West Hartlepool's Lister Street School found a home at Mulgrave Castle, near Whitby. This is a mid 19th century building and the third to bear the name since the original 13th century castle was built. The evacuees were given a wing to themselves and even had servants looking after them. However, even though many of them experienced the luxury of hot running water for the first time, they felt lonely and missed their mums ever so much.

What started as just a routine August day at Middlesbrough station in 1942 ended in terror. A German daylight raid scored a direct hit on the station roof causing it to partially collapse, trapping a train underneath, crushing the coaches and wrecking the tank engine. Teesside with its massive iron and steel works, and chemical factories, was a prime target for the Luftwaffe and our defences went to considerable lengths to protect our industries and to deceive the Germans. Sadly, eight people died and 56 were injured in the raid on a dull Bank Holiday Monday, 3 August, 1942. It would appear that the local media did an excellent job of keeping the news from the Germans. Word spread and everyone in Middlesbrough knew what had happened, but as the result of a propaganda campaign by the British government, everyone kept quiet because 'Careless Talk Costs Lives'.

Unbelievably, within a few days of the bombing the platforms have been cleared and the tracks repaired so the first train could steam out. The photograph is a tribute to the phenomenal dedication and guts of the LNER staff who worked so tirelessly to make it happen. In an earlier bombing (left) Middlesbrough had taken a severe battering from the Luftwaffe and over 100 fires raged throughout the town at the peak of the raid. As we can see in this photograph taken the following day, the Leeds Hotel and Newbould's shop on Linthorpe Road were completely destroyed. A report from the time described how a fire officer and a colleague walked along the road in the aftermath of the attack. They were shocked, when, in the half-light they stood on what they believed to be a naked corpse, around 100 yards from Newboulds. Their relief was considerable when they realised that it was, in fact, half a pig which had flown through the air from the pie shop propelled by the force of the blast!

When the bombs fall from the sky they do not distinguish between industrial and private property, nor do they worry about whether it is your house or that of God. St Peter's Church, only the second Anglican church to be erected 'over the border', had served its parish with distinction since its consecration on 2 September, 1873. Built of plain brick in the English style, it acquired a more distinctive look in 1901 when the tower and spire, donated by Sir Raylton and Lady Dixon, were added. Although those additions were only partially damaged in one of the air raids in June 1940, the body of the church was completely wrecked. Parishioners stood around the shell on the following morning, scarcely able to believe their eyes at the sacrilege committed by Goering's pilots. For two years after the raid on St Peter's services were held in the church hall until the congregation transferred to St Hilda's. This was a coincidence, the two parishes having already combined in 1932. A new St Peter's Church Hall was put up at Thorntree, but vandalism badly affected it and the site was cleared in the late 1970s.

Left: No one liked wearing the gas masks, but young mothers with babies had a particularly difficult time during the Second World War, when masks were issued to all British civilians. There was a very real fear in Britain that German bombers would drop poison gas bombs. Babies, however, had special cradle-like respirators which would only be issued out if an emergency situation arose. Babies were put inside the case and when all the covering flaps were folded and the straps closed up. The baby was totally enclosed, fresh air was pumped in, using a hand pump, through a filter on the side ensuring the baby inhaled no gas. Mothers were greatly affected by the thought of their babies suffocating inside their gas masks.

Below: The picture of John Todd in uniform stood on the mantelpiece during the joiner's absence from home as he served king and country during the war. It was now early January in 1947 and he had been demobbed and it was time to get back to normal family life. Tea in the front room by the fire was something John had missed, but it was not easy for him or his Army mates to return to civvy street. Some had children who hardly recognised them and others were unlucky as they did not have wives or sweethearts who had waited faithfully for them. It took time to rebuild relationships, but most managed it all right.

PARKS & RECREATION

Above and below: Great Ayton gives the impression of being a sleepy little place, but its connection with Cook and his voyages of exploration in the Pacific mean that visitors beat a steady path to the monuments, visitor centre and museum that are dedicated to his memory. Even though tourists are focused upon things antipodean, they cannot help but be entranced by the gentle countryside environment that includes the lapping waters of the River Leven. This peaceful stretch of water rises on Kildale Moor before flowing west through here and on to join the Tees at Yarm. Children take part in a special 'Captain Cook Day' every year. It is usually held on 27 October, the great man's birthday. Model boats, some with a passing likeness

to the Endeavour or the Resolution, are raced by kiddies along the Leven. Cook lived in the village for about eight years before leaving for Staithes. The population of Great Ayton is about 5,000 and boasts two village greens. High Green is in the centre, while Low Green can be found at the riverside. Great Ayton was mentioned in the Domesday Book and, in earlier days, was known for its tanning, brewing and linen making. Whinstone, ironstone, alum and jet were also dug from the ground in this vicinity, though farming has continued to be important to the local economy over countless generations.

Below and right: Albert Park contains quite a few statues, memorials and formal structures. A statue to Brian Clough, the much respected centre forward and great manager, is one of the more recent to have joined such diverse elements as a Crimean War cannon, Captain Cook carving and Boer War obelisk. The main entrance to the park was through a pair of attractively ornate gates, though these have been replaced in more recent times by sturdier ones. The original gates were paid for by the park's benefactor, Henry Bolckow, who bought them at an

exhibition in York. In the pre-First World War picture, the cast iron clock was erected here as a gift from Alderman Thomas Sanderson JP. It dates from around the start of the 20th century and includes a column with four engaged shafts. Behind it is West Lodge which used to be the park curator's house, it was built two years before the park opened. The 1876 sundial to the right was another of Bolckow's gifts and allows you to read the time in New York and Melbourne. The impressive Cenotaph that stands just outside the Linthorpe Road entrance was unveiled in 1922, close to the Dorman Museum. Behind it are two walls containing 24 panels. The names of those who fell in the 1914-18 War are inscribed on them. There is a horrific total of over 3,000 entries. Lest we forget.

Above and below: Covering about 100 acres, Albert Park is a major Middlesbrough amenity. It boasts a variety of interests for people of all ages, from roller skating to boating and tennis to bowls. There are gardens to delight, water features to admire and a bandstand to enjoy. The land was bought for about £30,000 and donated to the town by Henry Bolckow in 1868. As with many wealthy Victorian industrialists and entrepreneurs, he was keen in contributing to a society that had provided him

with such prosperity. Initially dubbed 'People's Park', it soon took on the name of Queen Victoria's consort who had died in 1861. The peaceful nature of the waters and the sight of the pretty flowers and elegant fountain, pictured in 1956, are quite soothing. But, it has seldom been this quiet. Normally, the sound of children's laughter echoes across the vista. Back in the days of the last war, this was one of the places where it was recommended for us to spend our 'Holidays at Home'. This was a government-inspired and council-run programme designed to save fuel supplies and boost morale. Games, sports and competitions were arranged in popular locations, such as parks, and locals encouraged to have fun for the most modest outlay.

Below: It is doubtful that any future giants of the art world came from this class at Middlesbrough High School for Boys, but it would not have been for the want of trying. However, quite what was supposed to be so inspirational about producing a representation of a bucket and shovel is hard to put into words. Perhaps the idea was to promote an early Damien Hurst rather than a David Hockney. The Albert Road school, dating back to 1877, was later sited on Marton Road and catered for over 600 pupils at its peak in the 1960s. In 1967, it merged with the parallel girls' school. It was developed into Middlesbrough and Marton Sixth Form College in 1974 and was consolidated, earlier this century, into Middlesbrough College and the Marton Road site largely given over to housing.

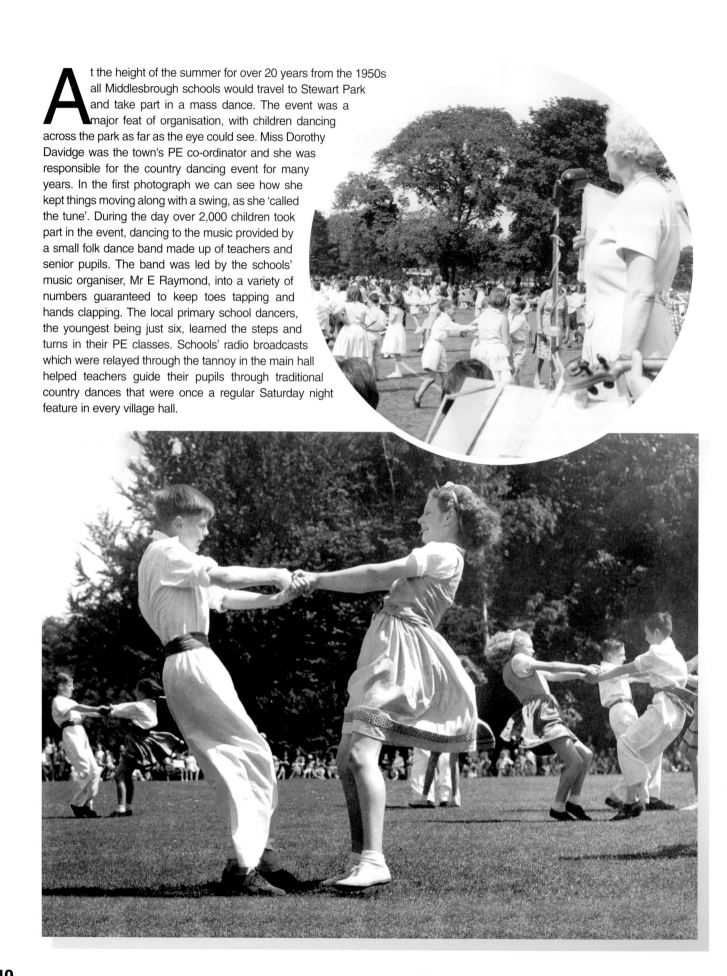

At the height of the summer for over 20 years from the 1950s all Middlesbrough schools would travel to Stewart Park and take part in a mass dance. The event was a major feat of organisation, with children dancing across the park as far as the eye could see. Miss Dorothy Davidge was the town's PE co-ordinator and she was responsible for the country dancing event for many years. In the first photograph we can see how she kept things moving along with a swing, as she 'called the tune'. During the day over 2,000 children took part in the event, dancing to the music provided by a small folk dance band made up of teachers and senior pupils. The band was led by the schools' music organiser, Mr E Raymond, into a variety of numbers guaranteed to keep toes tapping and hands clapping. The local primary school dancers, the youngest being just six, learned the steps and turns in their PE classes. Schools' radio broadcasts which were relayed through the tannoy in the main hall helped teachers guide their pupils through traditional country dances that were once a regular Saturday night feature in every village hall.

Originally opened as the Regal Cinema on 22 April, 1935, it was taken over by Oscar Deutsch Ltd in 1944 and re-named the Odeon in March 1945. One of the most popular cinemas in Stockton, it also had a very well attended and busy restaurant. The building was apparently closed because of a structural problem in 1966. A replacement was built on the same site two years after the demolition of the previous building. The luxurious new cinema opened with Julie Andrews in 'Thoroughly Modern Millie' on 25 April,1968. The rise in popularity of colour TV brought about a trend of declining cinema audiences across the country and the Stockton Odeon was no exception. This led to its closure in October 1981. Cinemas have a special place in the affections of many Stockton couples who will have fond memories of their 'courting days' and nervous first dates at venues like the Odeon.

BUILDINGS, MONUMENTS & BRIDGES

Above and below: The earliest picture of this group dates from 1909. Victoria Park and its bandstand (below) were situated on the site of a former cattle market. The land was also used for a variety of entertainments which included a skating rink and the venue for a circus. The area was developed into an attractive garden and promenade in 1901. Sir Samuel Sadler (1842-1911), a local MP and industrialist, took charge at the inauguration as the amenity was donated to the public.

Nicknamed 'the Colonel', a statue to him showing the thrice mayor in ceremonial robes was erected near the Albert Road entrance in 1913. Sculpted by Edouard Lanteri, the bronze figure sits on a pink marble pedestal. The Police Band regularly played at the bandstand in that first decade of the last century. The pathways and seats provided pleasant places from which to view Middlesbrough Town Hall and the Municipal Buildings. The foundation stone was laid in 1883 and the building work took another five years to complete at a cost in the region of £130,000. Designed by Darlington architect G G Hoskins, an official opening ceremony was held on 23 January, 1889. The Prince and Princess of Wales presided as the ceremonial ribbon was cut. They would later be elevated to King Edward VII and Queen Alexandra on the demise of Queen Victoria. This Town Hall replaced the one built in earlier times near where the Transporter Bridge can be found. There is little trace, other than the clock tower later used as a community centre, of Middlesbrough's initial growth from a hamlet into a town on the banks of the Tees. This was when Joseph Pease and a group of Quaker businessmen helped lay out four streets leading to the market square and oversaw the extension of the Darlington-Stockton railway to Middlesbrough.

Above: In this popular view of the Town hall from the 1920s, we can see the statue of John Vaughan in the foreground. We can estimate the date as this statue used to stand near Middlesbrough Railway Station so clearly the photograph was taken after its transfer to Victoria Square. The bandstand is also interesting because there appears to be a kiosk-like structure incorporated within it, which is not shown in earlier photographs.

Right: The Royal Exchange situated at the corner of Wilson Street is featured here in a photograph from September 1938. The boards outside the building advertise luncheons and

teas at 'moderate prices', though it is unlikely that many of the men seen on the corner of the street would have been able to afford them. The Royal Exchange Buildings date from 1868, though they replaced an earlier facility which was first opened in 1838. Sadly, the fine old building was pulled down in the mid-1980s to make way for a new road system. When it was built it cost the considerable sum of £28,000 - more than had been anticipated at the time, and the construction of a grand tower which had been part of the original design had to be abandoned due to the lack of funds. The Exchange was the place where people trading in iron, steel and other locally-produced commodities would meet on Tuesdays and Fridays to negotiate the price of these goods, all of which were crucial to the local economy.

where it was reassembled. The following year, this monument was presented to Great Ayton by W Russell Grimwade, the astute Aussie businessman who had engineered the removal of a bit of British heritage.

Right: Sir Hugh Bell (1844-1931) was a former mayor of Middlesbrough, High Sheriff of Durham and Lord Lieutenant of the North Riding. This school, overlooking Victoria Square on Grange Road, was named after him and he performed the opening ceremony in 1892. There were two schools within one as the building became home to separate establishments for boys and girls until closure in the 1960s. Both establishments developed reputations for strict discipline. One maths teacher, 'Buller' Madden, was renowned for teaching a class of boys who were not permitted to utter a word unless asked a direct question. The cane was liberally in use, it seems. Girls were told by one headmistress that going to the pictures or dances was not to be recommended and that they should not read sensationalist literature. Happy days!

Above and right: Situated at the foot of the Cleveland Hills and on the edge of the North York Moors, Great Ayton is a small village that attracts coachloads of tourists because of its connection with that intrepid explorer of the South Seas, Captain James Cook. However, the pictured religious building, Christ Church, dates from after his time as it originated in 1876. A war memorial inscribed 'Faithful unto death' stands to its right. It is dedicated to those who died in the Great War of 1914-18. The monument on Easby Lane, opposite the attractive period cottages on Race Terrace, is hewn from rocks from Cape Everard, near Point Hicks, in the Australian state of Victoria. This was where Lieutenant Zachary Hicks, a colleague of the then Lieutenant Cook on the HMS Endeavour, sighted land in April 1770. Cook was born in Marton in 1728, moving to Great Ayton in 1736. He was killed in what is now Hawaii in 1779. In 1933, the Cook family cottage that had been on this site was dismantled and shipped out to Fitzroy Park, Melbourne,

Below: The old Post Office suffered at the hands of developers in the 1970s and part of it was lost to the demolition crews. It now includes the home of the Teesside Archives. The statue of Henry Bolckow (1806-1878), sculpted by D W Stevenson, was unveiled in Exchange Square in 1881. It commemorated the man thought by many to be a leading figure in the founding of modern Middlesbrough. Born in Germany, he came to England in his late teens and was soon involved in the rapidly expanding ironworking industry. His statue was moved to Albert Park in 1924, but replaced close to its original home in 1986.

Above and below: It is great to see the railway station and Zetland Road in their original state. The station we know today was officially opened for passengers in 1877. Designed by the North Eastern Railway's principal architect, William Peachey, it was described at the time as one of the largest and finest on the North Eastern system and remains today as one of the few remaining Victorian public buildings in the town. Clearly seen in this photograph is the ornate arched roof of the original building. Although subsequently repaired, the building was destroyed by the Luftwaffe in 1942. Some locals may say that more damage was achieved by town planners in the 1960s when a huge office block called Zetland House was built in the middle of the station building. Fortunately, this was demolished in 2006 and the station has been restored to something like its former appearance.

Right: The diversion around Park Road North was completed in October 1954 and this was part of the resultant scene on 17 November. The picture is dominated by the two structures that still hold pride of place here almost sixty years on. Thousand have gathered around the Cenotaph to lay wreaths and say prayers each year since it was dedicated on 11 November, 1922. The £11,000 Aberdeen granite memorial was unveiled by the deputy mayor, Councillor J G Pallister, accompanied by two blind war veterans whose presence heightened the sadness of the proceedings. The Cenotaph is close to the main entrance to Albert Park where the Dorman Memorial Museum was built on the east side of Linthorpe Road at a cost of £15,000. It was handed over to the mayor, Councillor A C Dorman, by his father on 1 July, 1904. Colonel J Hoole performed the official opening ceremony as the museum was dedicated to the memory of the mayor's brother, A L Dorman, a member of the Green Howards, killed in the Boer War. The Dorman Museum developed through the last century to the level at which it could boast that it had something for everyone. In March 2011, the Dorman Memorial Museum was given the honour of displaying the Middlesbrough meteorite (loaned from the Yorkshire Museum). This was the first time the 3.3 lb meteorite had been put on display in the town since it fell to Earth in March 1881.

Body and soul come together in this picture, taken on 9 April, 1962. The church provided an opportunity for meditation, the pub gave relaxation and the bridge transportation. St Hilda's Parish Church was built with seating for 600 worshippers and a service of consecration was held in 1840. The addition of a new gallery in 1861 offered places for another 300 to give thanks to God and those who had given so generously towards its building costs. These had been raised by public subscription, with the land being freely given by Joseph Pease and 'The Owners' of the Middlesbrough Estate. At the time of this scene St Hilda's was struggling to continue its life as a vibrant parish church As the population had moved away to newer areas the congregation dwindled. The clergy at All Saints, Linthorpe Road, took over the running of St Hilda's until its demolition in 1970. In the distance, on North Street, the man and van are outside the Middlesbrough Hotel. Built on the site of an ancient Benedictine priory, it had been a popular watering hole since 1846. Landlords used to joke that it was more of a holy watering hole, because of its religious connections! The Middlesbrough Hotel was a handy stopping off place for those en route to or from the Transporter Bridge, seen behind and above North Street.

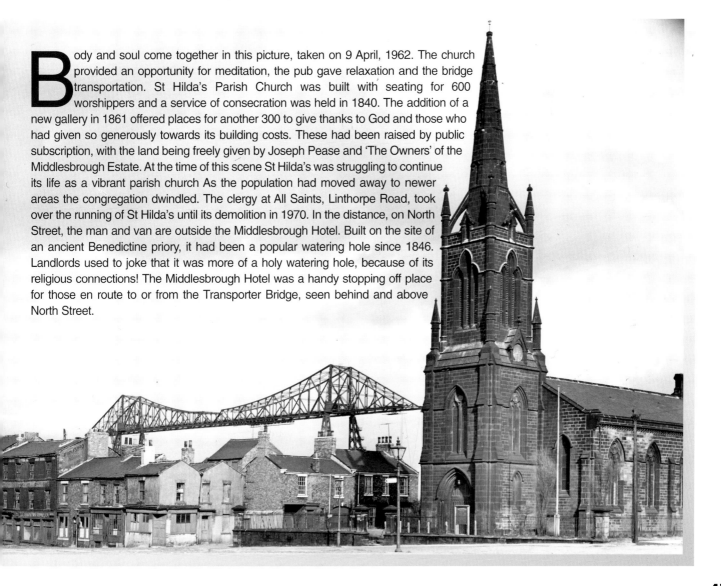

This is a typical scene from the High Street in Stockton, dating from around 1950. The Town Hall, or Town House as it is traditionally known, has been the hub of the action in Stockton, from its position in the centre of the town's High Street, for the last 276 years. The original building was erected on the site of a smithy and later extended to include hipped pantiled roofs, with central clock tower and belfry. Built in 1735, in the Dutch style, it shows the importance of the town at that time, and this is also reflected in similar buildings still standing in nearby Norton and Yarm. It is one of the oldest in the country still used for its original purpose and was granted Grade II* listed status in 1951. In the distance is the Parish Church and in the foreground is the Doric Column. This is a grade II listed monument and is thought to be the largest 'Market Cross' in the region. Unveiled in 1768, it stands eight metres high and cost the princely sum of £45 to build. This area around the Town Hall was a hive of activity with a market held three times a week, authorised by a Charter of the Bishop of Durham in 1310.

K Home International
Engineering Excellence Worldwide

K Home International Ltd, based at Ingram House, Allensway, Thornaby, Stockton-on-Tees, provides comprehensive world class engineering design solutions from concept through to beneficial operation for developers and operators of process and infrastructure projects. Integration of current Health, Safety and Environmental legislation into all project design is fundamental to the firm's success.

The company was founded in the North East of England in the early 1970s with the aim of providing an engineering design, project and construction management service that delivered the most appropriate and effective solutions for its clients.

Today the firm, which remains privately-owned, operates around the world and works within a broad range of industrial sectors. By applying a multi-disciplinary approach, KHI offers integrated projects teams to both local and global clients.

Throughout its years in business the firm has gained an enviable reputation for delivering safe, compliant and consistently

productive capital projects. KHI is committed to continuous improvement and building sustainability into all aspects and phases of it work.

What was then simply named K Home Engineering Limited was first registered with Companies House on 25 November, 1973.

The firm's first premises were Thornaby House, in Thornaby, overlooking the River Tees near to the Victoria Bridge.

In 1975, the company moved a short distance to the Chapel Street office which used to be part of the Head Wrightson offices on what is now Teesdale.

Two years later the company moved again, this time to Thornaby New Town, over the road from the area's biggest supermarket Woolco, now ASDA. The new office, Ingram House, is still the main location for the company.

Top: Home International Ltd's Ingram House, Stockton-on-Tees, premises. **Left:** Founder, Ken Home (right), receives the Teesside Business Executive of the Year Award for 1997.

In 2004, the company changed its name to K Home International in recognition of the world-wide spread of its project work.

By then the firm and its founder had already received widespread recognition. In 1994 the company had won the Teesside Company of the Year Award. In 1997, company founder Ken Home won the Teesside Business Executive of the Year Award. Again, in 2003, the company won the Teesside, and then the North East, Company of the Year. In both 1998 and 2005 the company won the Queen's Award for Export.

In 2003, Ken received the OBE for services to industry in Teesside, a very proud day for him and his family. The ceremony at Buckingham Palace was attended by Ken, his wife Judy and two of their children.

Most recently, K Home International Limited has had its approach to the prevention of accidents and ill health recognised in the RoSPA Occupational Health and Safety Awards 2012. It won a Gold Award in the annual scheme, which dates back to 1956 and is the largest and longest-running awards programme of its kind in the UK.

But how did Ken Home, ably supported by his wife, come to found this prestigious firm?

Ken and Judy had five young children when the company started, so it was a brave move to make. But they both had faith in Ken's ability to make a go of it, and a strong desire to do something for themselves.

Ken had previously been a director of Head Wrightson, the local firm which once employed nearly 6,000 people and mostly made boilers and other heavy engineering. Its factory covered 68 acres until its closure in 1987.

During his time at Head Wrightson, he had travelled to many parts of the world working on projects, or tendering for work, in heavy industries such as iron and steel, aluminium smelting, copper plants, and energy from waste plants.

Whilst at Head Wrightson, he had been the project director for a new aluminium smelter built in Invergordon, Scotland. His experience there and the friendships he made on that project would prove significant in the future of K Home Engineering Ltd.

Top left: Ken Home receives his OBE from Her Majesty the Queen in 2003. *Above:* The Queen's Award presentation in 2005. *Below:* A new aluminium smelter built in Invergordon, Scotland, for which Ken home was project director during his time at Head Wrightson.

Computer-aided design replaced hand drawn designs, with the last drawing board finally leaving the office in the early 1990s.

The company invested in some of the first 3-dimensional model systems. Training of staff was an issue, however, because as soon as they had been trained many would leave to use their new found skills elsewhere. Today, computers are essential for the running of the business. Most design is done in 3-D with high quality graphics.

Technology in communications has also changed the way the business operates. When fax machines came out these were thought of as a huge development in helping communication, especially when working on overseas projects.

In the mid-nineties when the company was doing a lot of work in the Middle East most drawings and other documents had to be hand carried between Teesside and the site; then the company invested in a dedicated IT link between locations and information could be sent electronically.

Needless to say, over the 40 years of doing business the company has experienced several harsh recessions and cycles in the industrial market. However, Ken's business

Initially there was only Ken working in the new company. After the first month, however, Ken had won sufficient orders to employ four staff. Salaries in 1973 amounted to just £250 a month.

Ken took on people he knew and trusted – his first member of staff was Don Fullalove who joined the firm one month after its start; he stayed with the company until he retired 25 years later. By the end of the first year staff numbers were 14.

The company grew organically through successful winning and delivery of projects, peaking at 400 people.

In 1975, Ken took on Ted Bowes, who became a business partner and trusted friend. Ted would stay with the company until retirement in the mid-1990s.

In those early days all design was done on drawing boards and the design office was a sea of boards. To keep costs down in the early days Ken went to Lithgow's auction house in Stokesley to buy second hand drawing boards.

In such a technical business, however, Ken always understood the need to keep investing in technology to provide the best service possible to clients.

This page: Services provided by K Home International: Construction Management (top left), Project Cost Estimating, Control & Procurement (left) and Project Management & Risk Management (below).

Another early overseas job was in Pakistan. Working in conjunction with German technology company Uhde the company designed and managed the construction of a chemical plant there.

In the early nineties the company was invited to bid for some work on an aluminium smelter in Dubai, through one of Ken's old colleagues on the Invergorden project. What started as a relatively small piece of work eventually turned into a major project. This helped raise the profile of the company internationally, and secured its reputation in a niche area of business as a global player.

At the same time as working in the desert heat of Dubai the company was also building a smelter in Iceland, so the extremes of weather were exceptional.

The company has worked in many other countries, but focusing on the Middle East with projects in Abu Dhabi, Qatar, Bahrain, Kuwait and Oman. Other project locations include Trinidad, Venezuela, Mexico, Nova Scotia, Borneo and Malaysia.

prudence allowed the firm to survive through those challenges, when many other companies failed. Ken's strategy was always to build a sustainable business which was robust, rather than focusing on short term gain.

At one point, ICI accounted for 90% of the company's business. As ICI fragmented and the number of plants on Teesside reduced this became a challenge to work with new clients and find alternative sources of work.

The success and longevity of the business is in no small part due to the principles of how Ken ran the business and these still guide the philosophy of the company today: honesty, integrity, looking after staff, and paying suppliers on time.

Meanwhile, down the years the company has been to some far flung places. The first overseas job was in Hong Kong. Ken went on a Trade Mission to Hong Kong and managed to secure some work on a cement facility on the strength of the company's expertise in material handling. The contacts in Hong Kong went on to yield some interesting work, including a system for storing money in the vault at Hong Kong and Shanghai Bank.

Another Trade Mission, this time to Saudi Arabia, led to several projects in the desert including a military camp near the Yemeni border and a chemical plant. Business was conducted in an unusual fashion - every month Ken had to visit the client in Saudi where he was paid in cash. When this first happened he asked what he should do with a bag full of cash and he was sent to the local money lender in the souk who would give Ken a cheque which he could bank.

This page: *More services provided by the company: Multi-Discipline Engineering, Detail Design and 3D Modelling (top left) and Feasibility Studies & Front End Engineering Design (below).*

Today, the company continues to focus on its core business, continually improving and extending the range of services it offers to the industrial project sector.

In Teesside the company works with the chemical industry, what used to be predominantly ICI and is now a myriad of international blue chip companies. It also works in the international mining and metals industry for large multinationals. At the other end of the scale, the company also works for small start-up businesses, especially in new industries such as renewable energy.

It is, however, large, world-class projects that the company's name has become most associated with. These include the Nordural aluminium smelter in Iceland, built in a record time of 13 months; the Sea Dragon drilling rig was one of the most advanced of its type; and the electrolyte plant at Lucite's Cassel Works in Billingham, which produces battery components for electric vehicles.

KHI carried out many projects from its office in Trinidad. The most prestigious was a project to achieve a significant reduction in greenhouse gases by the reduction/elimination of flaring and venting of Hydrocarbon gases, on BP Trinidad & Tobago Facilities, both offshore and onshore.

When Dubai went through its extraordinary construction boom in at the beginning of the century the company's office there was involved in big infrastructure projects such as district cooling plants and distribution networks on the man-made 'Palm' islands. The company provided project and construction management services for multiple sky scrapers and also the world-class Atlantis Hotel.

As for involvement in the local community, the firm actively supports local youth sports teams including squash, basket ball, football, cycling and cricket. The company also supports local charities including St John Ambulance, Cleveland Mountain Rescue and local hospices. The firm has been particularly inspired by the hospice started by Mary Butterwick. Mary's story of creating a professional and dedicated organisation was very similar to Ken Home's.

Top left, left and top right: *A selection of Home International projects: the Sea Dragon drilling rig (top left), the Atlantis Hotel in Dubai (left) and Project Titan for local firm Huntsman Tioxide (top right).* **Above right:** *A 3D model of a Home International project created with CAD.*

The firm is still an independent family owned business with a focus on providing quality service in a personalised way. The company operates in a famously friendly way, which is why many employees are keen to return when they have left. As the company celebrates its 40th birthday in 2013, it will also celebrate several long serving members of staff who have been with the company for 25 years.

The size and structure means that the company can be flexible in how it works with clients, and also be responsive with no large decision-making hierarchy to get through. The same quality and breadth of services as many much larger competitors is offered, but delivered in a more effective way.

In the late 1990s, Ken's two sons, Andrew and Michael, joined the business. One of Ken's grandchildren now works in the business too.

The current Board of Directors comprises Andrew Home, Michael Home, Peter Kay and Lee Anderson. Founder Ken Home still acts in an advisory role as Company Chairman.

Top left: *A grain-based ethyl alcohol plant for Royal Nedalco, Manchester.* **Above:** *The Board of Directors. From left: Lee Anderson and Peter Kay (standing), and Michael Home and Andrew Home (seated).* **Below:** *Andrew Home and Peter Kay with new company name sign.*

ENTERTAINMENT, LEISURE & CELEBRATIONS

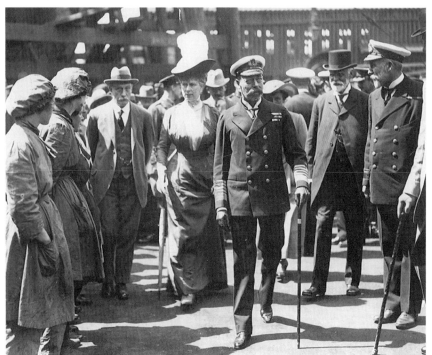

Right: Coronation Day in 1937 was a good enough excuse for a fancy dress competition - judged by the Mayor of Middlesbrough himself. Here 'Prince Charming' is seen being congratulated by the Mayor on his achievement while other children and the Lady Mayoress look on. The whole of Middlesbrough was decorated with flags, flowers and bunting as the town rejoiced at the Coronation of their new king. The people of Middlesbrough have always demonstrated strong affection for the royal family and this has been rewarded by more than the town's fair share of royal visits over the years.

Above and right: Teesside was very proud to receive a Royal visit from the King and Queen in June 1917. King George V and Queen Mary came to Middlesbrough as part of an extensive tour of the great shipbuiding establishments of the Tees, Wear, Tyne and Humber. At the time, this was a very flattering tribute to the industries of the Northeast and believed to be the first visit to Teesside by a reigning monarch. In this photograph we can see the Royal couple receiving a very characteristic, warm hearted welcome from the shipyard workers. The King wears his naval uniform, but most of the workers, including female munitions workers, are in their regular work clothes. The visit was clearly intended to be as informal as possible. There is little apparent crowd control but the Royal couple look unconcerned. The King's main objective was to learn first-hand the story of the magnificent achievements of Britain's industrial army in the production of the infinite variety of ships and materials, dubbed as "munitions of war", and to see for himself the arduous working conditions. The initial inspection was of the shipyards of the South Bank and Middlesbrough and afterwards on to Stockton.

Below: This procession along Albert Road took place on the Sunday immediately following Corpus Christi, from its inception by Bishop Lacy in 1925 until 1971. The event attracted thousands onto the streets every year to watch the parade go by. A police car led the way, followed by the Cathedral band, a cross bearer, scouts, schoolchildren from St Mary's, St Philomena's, and others, Young Christian Workers, altar boys, priests, nuns and the faithful. These devout children displayed their hearts and their beliefs on their sleeves in 1966. Corpus Christi is an important feast day in the church calendar, especially honoured by the Catholic Church. Literally translated as 'body of Christ' the festival is a special commemoration of the communion host, the procession being the only occasion when the Eucharist is paraded in public.

This page: Tyne Street, in the old town, connected Lower Feversham Street and Bridge Street East. These are the homes that our grandparents possibly grew up in, back to back terraces and, for some, a communal street tap as many houses did not have running water. There was not even a back yard to hang out the washing, so it was strung across the street. Housing conditions appear primitive to us today, cocooned in our centrally heated homes and aided by modern electrical appliances. What they did have in bucket loads was community spirit. Everyone knew everyone else and they looked out for each other as one big family.

The building that we can see at the far end of the street was an important entertainment centre, the grandly named Oxford Music Hall and Palace of Varieties. It was situated on Rostock Terrace and Richard Weighell was one of its early owners. He was a racehorse breeder and local politician who was the town mayor in 1885. This music hall opened on 9 August, 1867, and audiences were entertained by Alvante and Petro Athos on the flying trapeze. More famous names than those trod the boards in later years. Dan Leno, the first music hall artist to appear at a Royal Command Performance, starred here, Harry Houdini performed escapology, Harry Lauder sang and Charlie Chaplin performed routines to packed houses. Looking to be accepted as more upmarket, it was renamed simply in 1900 as the Oxford Theatre. In later life it became a warehouse and was used by the Diamond Grit works before falling victim to a bombing raid in 1940 and was subsequently demolished.

Rght: How excited must this group of young lads have been, to play football with one of Middlesbrough's all time greats, Wilf Mannion. The playing surface on this particular street in Middlesbrough doesn't look ideal, but who cares when you can play against one of your local idols. A football and jumpers for posts is all you need to get started. A young girl on the sidelines looks as though she may be holding the half time drinks. Could any of these lads have become Boro stars of the future? When this photograph was taken in November 1951, Mannion had just retired from the national team, having been capped by England 26 times. He was a member of the England squad in the 1950 World Cup Finals in Brazil, but the team did not qualify from their group. He did however score a goal in Englands first match against Chile.

Left: Her Majesty Queen Elizabeth is smiling as she alights from the entrance of a Mobile Catering Canteen in Albert Park, on 19 August, 1941. The Queen Mother, as she later became affectionately known, is being assisted by Councillor Sir William Crosthwaite J.P the Mayor of Middlesbrough, on a morale boosting tour of the North East during the Second World War. The royal couple were inspecting the Civil Defence Services in the area and here the Queen was looking at the vehicle which was designed to provide emergency catering in the event of disruption to normal arrangements in the aftermath of a bombing raid. The mobile canteen was presented to the people of Middlesbrough by Lady Crosthwaite in June 1941.

"Hey mister what you got there"?! The gentleman replied, "It's the Crown Jewels". Not the real ones, of course, as they have been locked up in the Tower of London since 1303, after they were stolen from Westminster Abbey. Charles Elston, of Stockton-on-Tees is in fact holding a replica of the Tudor State Crown. The real one has an approximate value today of £1.7 million. The girls are clearly on their best behaviour as they angle to get a closer look. It is believed Mr Elston was a jeweller who had devoted 15 years to creating a replica of the Crown Jewels, and they took pride of place at the 1951 Festival of Britain.

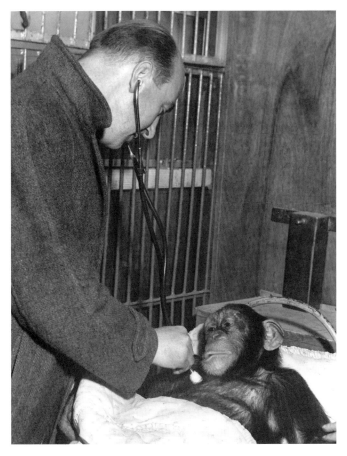

Left: Joey, the chimp at Billy Smart's Circus in Middlesborough in April, 1954, is ill with a chest complaint and cannot appear in the ring. So each morning, Dr. H K Seiser, calls in to give him a run-over with his stethoscope. Joey was one of the first six chimpanzees to be trained at Billy Smart's Circus along with the rest of the troupe that included Dean, Dido, Miny, Big Boy and Charlie.They were trained by German-born Baptist Schreiber, a noted chimpanzee trainer who came to Britain in 1953 and also claimed to have trained Ham, the first chimp sent into space. Three months before Alan Shepard's flight in 1961, the "chimponaut" went into orbit and returned safely.

Below: Queen Elizabeth II turns to smile and waves to the crowd as she leaves the Town Hall in Middlesbrough, accompanied by the Mayor, Alderman F. Manton. The Queen and the Duke of Edinburgh visited Middlesbrough on 4 June, 1956, as part of a tour of the North East. The young Queen was extremely popular at this time, the visit coming just three years after her Coronation. The crowds turned out in their thousands, lining the streets and cheering as the royal party passed. Delighted crowds in Stockton also had the opportunity to greet the Queen as she visited the ICI chemical plant and Stockton town hall. At the time of the visit there was concern about the political situation in Suez, and within months a crisis would develop which resulted in an R.A.F bombing raid which threatened to take the country to the brink of another all-out war.

Above: Beauty contests became the standing dish at seaside resorts up and down the country after the Second World War. These contests were the new kind of entertainment for holidaymakers as the country moved on from the greyness and austerity of the 1940s. The more serious bathing belles of the 50s and 60s would turn up at the resorts on the Lancashire coast and parade in front of large holiday crowds. The beauties who entered the Redcar event had to be made of sterner stuff. The six girls seen in this picture from August 1960, on Redcar beach not only had to turn out in their swimming cossies, but they also had to hurdle a skipping rope whilst having their photograph taken. To be fair, the girls seem to be having fun, but it is not the type of occurrence you would be likely to see today.

Left: What's the best way to get a piano out of the Alma Hotel? Clearly the best way is to leave it to the professionals. A small crowd had gathered to watch removers from K.W. Deveraux and Sons as they ever so gently guided this piano out of the first floor window of the hotel in Dovecot Street in the late 1950s. Hanging over the ledge is Deveraux foreman, Wilfy Hall and watching on behind is founder of the firm Ken Deveraux. Waiting on the ground is Clifford 'Chippy' Almond, although his gaze seems to be taken by the girls in the adjoining premises. The dovecot which gave the street its name stood on the site of the Alma Hotel and the adjoining building from medieval times until 1839, when it was demolished.

Above: This looks more like a crowd scene at a football match rather than shoppers trying to get into the opening of Duncan the Tailors store, in High Street, Stockton. Inside the store was British actor Ted Lune, who was making a guest appearance for the publicity shots (inset). Lune is best known for portraying Private Len Bone in the TV series, 'The Army Game', a British sitcom that aired on ITV from 1957 to 1961. There is obviously no room left inside the shop, so the mounted policeman has been called to keep crowd trouble to a minimum. But what kind of trouble did they expect from this largely female audience.

Above and below: During the summer and autumn of 1963, The Beatles appeared twice in the Teesside area. On 25 June, 1963, they played at the Astoria Ballroom in Middlesbrough, and almost four months later they were driving their fans wild again when they took the stage at the Globe Theatre in Stockton. In between the two concerts The Beatles had become an unbelievable phenomenon as 'Beatlemania' began to grip the country. The 'Fab Four' had arrived… big time, and to the delight and excitement of these mainly female fans, seen here in this photograph at the Globe on 22 November, 1963. Every female teenager in Teesside wanted to see The Beatles and sing and scream along to the words of 'Please, Please Me',

'She Loves You' and 'Twist and Shout'. With seating for approximately 2,500 only at each performance at the Globe, inevitably, many were disappointed as tickets were like gold dust. If you were at the concert in Stockton you will probably remember the experience for the rest of your life, but ironically a much bigger and more tragic event was taking place in Dallas. They say that everyone can remember exactly where they were and what they were doing when they heard the news about the assassination of President Kennedy. You may well have been one of The Beatles' fans who came out of the concert on a high, only to be utterly devastated by the news that the President had been shot dead.

Below: Under normal circumstances you would have checked such a photo for images of a monarch, fluttering Union Jacks or bunting stretched across the roadway. Yet, all of this is absent. This street party had nothing to do with the end of a war, a coronation or a special anniversary. Middlesbrough folk were simply using 1 April, 1968, as an excuse to have a knees up. It had been announced that this was the day on which the new County Borough of Teesside had been created. This was part of the biggest municipal reorganisation outside London. Wow! Let's have some fun then. They had to be quick as there was more change on the way. In 1974, Teesside Borough was abolished and its parts allocated to Cleveland or Hartlepool.

Above: They are still going strong, some 50 years after a cover of Chuck Berry's 'Come On' gave them their first hit single. The Rolling Stones performed in Stockton in 1964 and posed with this young fan for a photo that must hold pride of place in her collection of pop memorabilia. Pictured from the left, at the back are Bill Wyman, Charlie Watts and Mick Jagger, with Brian Jones and Keith Richards at the front. The Rolling Stones were popular in Europe and then became successful in North America during the mid-1960s British Invasion. They were the main rivals to The Beatles in the 1960s and can still sell out huge venues today. The Rock and Roll Hall of Fame inducted the Rolling Stones in 1989, noting that "critical acclaim and popular consensus has accorded them the title of the "World's Greatest Rock and Roll Band.""

Facing page: Once it was all big bands and going to the dance hall for a waltz or quickstep with your sweetheart, but there was a musical revolution in the air in the 1960s. It ousted those playing under the baton of the likes of Joe Loss and Ted Heath,

replacing them with smaller piece combos or groups, as they came to be known. Guitars, drums and, perhaps, a keyboard swept away the brass and wind instruments of yesteryear. Each town or city had its own favourites. Further up the coast on Tyneside, the Animals, featuring the likes of Eric Burdon and Alan Price, followed the example of Hank Marvin and Bruce Welch of the Shadows and pursued successful careers in the business. But, their grounding had come in youth clubs, pubs and church halls. It was there that they practised their art and built stage acts that would see them develop a local following that would transfer to the big time.

Teesside made its own contribution to the pop music scene of the day. The Zephyrs hailed from Stockton and had a particularly strong following. There were hundreds and hundreds of budding stars trying to make it, but there was only room for a handful in that hall of fame. Other acts like the Crestas, the Avengers and the Tempests played to appreciative teenagers who packed the Empire Continental, Globe Theatre or James Finnigan Hall. The Blue Caps was another outfit that commanded respect. Formed in 1959 by drummer Mick Kemp,

Whiskey Mack at the beginning was Alan Jacques on guitar, Sandy Beach on vocals, Jim Sculley on guitar, Alan Bowles on drums, Trisha Jacques on vocals and Terry Bradley as the bass player.

there were several personnel changes before the established line up included guitarists Eric Whitehouse and the Peacocks, Charlie and Ian, fronted by Tony Martin on vocals. They rocked audiences for most of the Swinging 60s.

The Blue Caps, seen here early 1966, were thought to be the only Teesside band ever to perform on the main stage of the Globe Theatre in Stockton. The line up (left to right) is Les Bennet, Peter Embleton, Mick Kemp, Ian "Tex" Peacock and Eric Whitehouse.

The Blue Caps were sufficiently well regarded to be hired to back established stars such as Emile Ford, Jimmy Crawford and Screaming Lord Sutch. Later in the decade, Whiskey Mack (this page) built up a big following. Although a number of acts, such as the Honeycombs, the Applejacks and the Springfields, included a female in the ensemble, this was still something of a rarity. Whiskey Mack was fronted by the dishy Trisha Jacques,

backed by her husband Alan, Jim Sculley, Alan Bowles and the delightfully named Sandy Beach. The group played cover versions of hit songs, but also developed a fine all round cabaret routine that got them a varied set of bookings. Trisha's good looks helped the performances, especially when she forgot to put on her hot pants during one quick costume change!

When the beat boom was in full swing, nights out in the northeast were times to be remembered. From the twist to the locomotion, from the hippy-hippy shake to the watusi; we had a ball.

A happy crowd near the duck pond in Ward Jackson Park again is Jim Sculley, Sandy Beach, Trisha Jacques, Alan Bowles and Alan Jacques.

Below: The queue at the ABC cinema on Borough Road appears to stretch round the corner on to Amber Street in this 1973 photograph. The film name above the entrance is for 'Westworld', starring Yul Brynner in a futuristic Western-themed amusement park. Westworld is credited as being the first film to use computer-generated images. Filmmakers were going through somewhat of a purple patch for brilliant blockbusters at the time with the release in 1973 of such classics as The Day of the Jackal, Enter the Dragon, American Graffiti, The Sting and The Exorcist. All were major box office hits and certainly worth queuing for. This popularity would not continue for more than a decade, however, as the ABC in Middlesbrough closed in 1983.

Below right: A photograph from 1976 showing Middlesbrough manager Jack Charlton with some of the children from Framwellgate Comprehensive School during a football coaching session. This was part of a Tyne Tees Television series of programmes named, 'Play Soccer - Jack Charlton's Way' made in the summer of '76. Apart from 'Big Jack' and the schoolboys, there were also Boro' trainees, one of who was, Stan Cummins, who went on to play professionally. Although Jack may have had his hands full with these young lads, he was certainly doing a good job at Middlesbrough in the league. He was offered the job as manager of second division Boro' on his 38th birthday in 1973, and led them to promotion back to the top flight in his first season. The team won by such a considerable margin that he was deservedly given the Manager Of The Year award.

Left: 'Come Fly with Me', as Frank Sinatra said in his 1958 song of the same name. In this photograph we can get a bird's eye view of the Rothmans sponsored aerobatic team practising over Teesside Airport on 14 March, 1975. The team was apparently the world's only civilian aerobatic team and can be seen here in their Pitts S2A biplane aircraft. Teesside Airport began its life as Royal Air Force Station Goosepool, and in 1941 became RAF bomber base Middleton St. George. In 1964 the airport was transferred from the military to local authorities. Later in the same year, the first scheduled flight from the airport flew passengers to Manchester. Significant redevelopment took place with the building of an airport hotel and passenger terminal, which was opened by Princess Margaretha of Sweden in 1966. By the time of this photograph the Teesside Airport had become a small but thriving hub serving both domestic and international destinations.

Above: You would be more likely to see ducks rather than young children in the pond at Norton Green these days. Obviously a sunny day, these young kids are having a whale of a time jumping from the circular steps of the fountain. Norton Green is at the northern edge of the High Street and this view will have changed very little in the last hundred years. The buildings surrounding the pond have only changed superficially in this picturesque village. At some point the telephone box in the background was added and the pond itself has been given a stonework edge. The pond is next to the B1274 and on the corner of High Street and Darlington Lane.

THE MARKET PLACE

These pictures give us an idea of the changing face of Stockton High Street from the early 20th century to the swinging 60s. The focal point is the area between the Town Hall and the Parish Church. The market which is one of the largest in the UK and many local readers will have bought goods from one of the 150 plus stalls, held every Wednesday and Saturday. A smaller market was opened in 1979 each Friday. The earliest photograph, on the left, was probably taken from Bishop Street in the 1890s, as it appears to pre-date electric trams that came into service in 1898. In the next image, chronologically, it is obvious that the motor had begun to dominate the scene in the middle of the last century. Private

motoring was no longer the preserve of the middle classes as affordable models came within the reach of ordinary families. Before long, car ownership was the norm rather than the exception. The white building behind the Parish Church is The Castle & Anchor public house, on the corner of Church Road. In 2010 the market reached an astonishing 700 year anniversary after the then Bishop of Durham Anthony Bec had granted the good townsfolk of Stockton permission to hold a market each Wednesday 'in perpetuity', back in 1310. It was still as popular as ever as we can see in the main photograph from the early 1960s. Either side of the High Street many of the businesses will be recognisable to the shoppers of today. On the left we can see The Welcut Tailors Ltd occupies the position on the corner of Victoria Buildings. On the opposite side we can see competion from Weaver and Weaver and next door is Marks & Spencers. Just further along we can see the new Littlewoooods store taking shape. Other stores on the street included, Stead & Simpson, Blacketts, H. Samuel and Hepworths, to name but a few.

Top left and left: It is sad to see the heart old Middlesbrough so derelict now when it was once such a busy, vibrant area. Open land and low cost housing have replaced Market Place. St Hilda's Church, with its 120 foot spire, was designed by J and B Green of Newcastle and opened on the site of a former 12th century Benedictine priory in 1840. The consecration was carried out by Dr E Maltby, the Bishop of Durham. It was funded by Joseph Pease, the railway pioneer. The church was demolished in 1969 and its bells incorporated into a campanile at the junction of Linthorpe Road and Grange Road. The old Town Hall was designed in an Italianate style by W L Moffatt of Doncaster in 1846. Only the graffiti covered tower remains today, looking forlorn and neglected. A few other buildings in the area, such as the Exchange and the old National Provincial Bank, given over to

the Cleveland Club in 1948 and now called Gibson House, offer a tenuous link with former glories. This latter building was erected on the site of the former home of John Gilbert Holmes, the town's first shipbuilder. It was built for the bank in 1872 by John Gibson. The house on the opposite side of Cleveland Street has a plaque recalling that Henry Bolckow and John Vaughan, founders of the local iron trade, lived there from 1841 to 1860. They formed a formidable partnership. By 1864, the company capital stood at £2.5 million making it the largest ever formed.

Above: In Stockton, fish was on sale all along the road from Little Brown Street to Ramsgate in 1920. This was hardly surprising since access to the local fishing boats was a matter of yards away. Here, on High Street, the crab and winkle stalls were situated close to the Shambles.

Right: Newhouses Corner, at the junction of Linthorpe Road and Corporation Road, has always been a popular spot for local shoppers. It originally served as the main link between the township of Middlesbrough and Linthorpe village. Newhouses store, was something of an institution in the town and generations of Middlebrough families will have fond memories of visiting over the years. Later the company was taken over by the Debenhams organisation. Across the way, Burton, 'the tailor of taste' as they liked to be known, also occupied a prime location from which to dress the male population of the area. The ornate lamp standard is a fabulous reminder of lighting in the 1950s and is a magnificent spectacle by comparison to their concrete counterparts of today.

Left and below: Postwar Linthorpe Road was a mainstay of the retail heart of the town, just as it is today, though the nature of shopping and the names above the doors have changed markedly. In the 1950s view, Ross's gents' outfitters dominated one side of the road. This store was established in 1904 and moved from here to Borough Road in 1961. The more recent photograph shows the once dominant Tower House that was part of the general store founded by Richard Archibald and Lawrence Wright in 1862, in Sussex Street. Wright's moved to the corner of Linthorpe Road and Grange Road in 1910. The building was demolished in the 1980s.

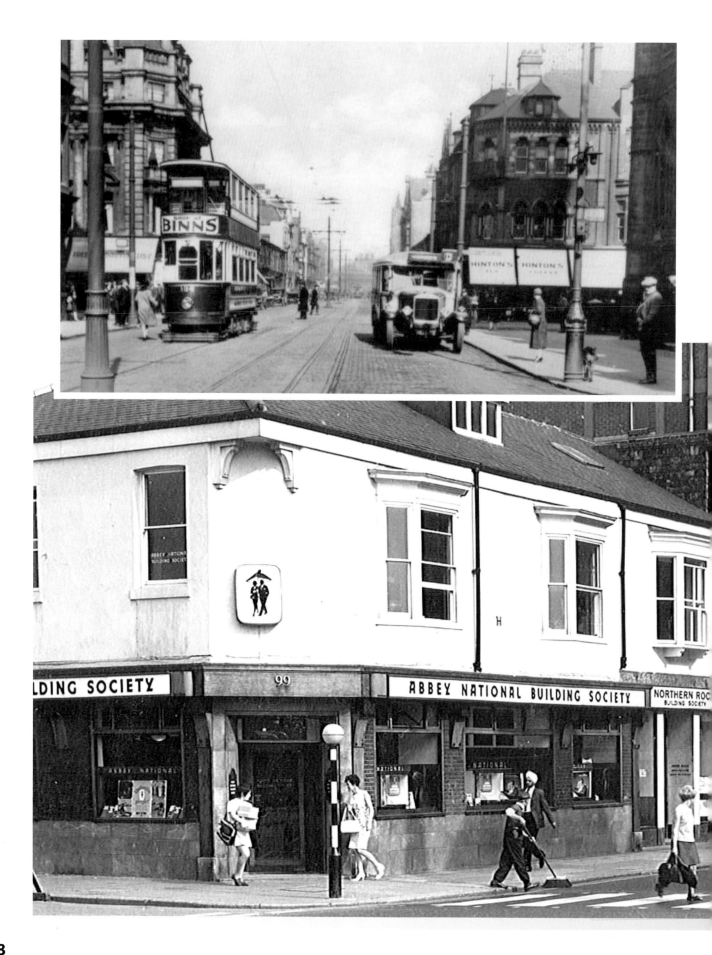

Left: The tram headed towards us along Albert Road advertised the name of one of our leading department stores. Over to the right, behind the bus, was another well-known chain store, situated at the corner with Corporation Street. It belonged to the grocer Amos Hinton (1844-1919). Born in Tring, he founded his business in Middlesbrough in 1871, moving to this site in 1890. Hinton became a leading local politician and keen supporter of the temperance movement. In 1886, he was the first Mayor to serve in the new Town Hall. The HSBC now occupies a more modern building on the site.

Below and right: Parts of Albert Road are now quite dark as the Cleveland Centre and Dundas Shopping Mall cast their shadows across the highway. Back in the late 1960s this part of town was a much lighter, brighter place in which to walk. The block of buildings towards which we are looking at was home to a number of financial concerns that included three building societies, the Abbey National, Northern Rock and the Leeds Permanent. These establishments did good business in providing the funds for mortgages that helped the home buying boom that had blossomed during this decade. Skirts may have been short, but cash was plentiful as we changed dreams into reality.

ALONG THE COAST

Even as early as the late 18th century, Quakers from the northeast region, many of them well heeled bankers, made Seaton Carew a popular place to come for a holiday. By the time Queen Victoria was settled on the British throne, bathing machines, based on designs used by pioneering swimmers in Scarborough, appeared on the beach. Gas lighting was introduced along the promenade and a new sea wall was constructed, helping to revitalise the village and turn it into a threat to the position Redcar enjoyed as a major resort on this stretch of coastline. These bathing machines, with their adverts for Beecham's famous pills, were photographed in August 1890. Notice the sailor outfits, so popular at the time, worn by several of the young boys. Three years earlier the local authorities had indulged in a fierce debate that the machines, segregated for male and female use, were placed too close together for the likes of those with stern views of Victorian modesty. One councillor thought that they should be sited 50 yards apart. Seaton Carew continued to attract holidaymakers well into the next century and its attractions included a new promenade that opened in 1905. In the inter-war years of the 1930s, day trippers enjoyed themselves in George Siddle's fairground and in the kiosks and cafés that abounded here.

Redcar was described at the start of the 18th century as 'a considerable fishing town'. It had some 500 inhabitants and, with its easily accessible beach, was already becoming a fashionable place for 'sea bathing' by the time the beginning of the next century was reached. Wind-blown sand often piled up outside the seafront cottages, but elsewhere efforts were made to keep the beaches neat and tidy in order to bring in an increasing number of visitors attracted here as the railway age took off in the mid-1800s. By the time the earliest of these photographs was taken, the population had increased to several thousand, most of whom relying on tourism or fishing for their incomes. Those coming here on holiday did not have far to travel from the foundries, mines, railways and shipyards of the northeast. At Redcar they could find an escape from the weary world of work for a week or two.

In 1900, Redcar promenade was little more than a strip of asphalt between the road and the sands. It was remodelled and extended and new amenities added to boost tourism. Zetland Estates rented out many of the seafront properties to tenants who took in paying guests.

They enjoyed the jollity of fairground rides that included a steam roundabout, though this attraction was not universally popular after dark as its noisy machinery kept children awake. Ladies strolled along the promenade in the early 1900s showing off their flowing, floor length dresses. By the time that their descendants were showing off their curves in bikinis, the British seaside break was in decline.

Continental package holidays became the name of the game from the 1960s onwards. In modern times, some regeneration of the front has taken place, though part of this is to do with sea defences. However, there are still small fishing and pleasure boats dotted along here. But, looking west today towards Coatham, we can see the Seaside Store and a Chinese takeaway opposite the helter skelter shaped vertical pier. That's progress.

There was much more to enjoy on the promenade and the sands. Live entertainment was everywhere, with pierrrots, clowns, jugglers, comedians, singers and magicians keeping spectators enthralled. Men in leotard styled bathing costumes and ladies heading off to bathing machines enjoyed the fun and freedom of it all. Kiddies laughed at the antics of performing dogs and were always amused by the mayhem of the Punch and Judy show. They were also thrilled to ride on one of Burniston's donkeys or take a dip in the open air pool that was built in 1930. Our great grandparents joined in with the songs performed by Grapho and Jackson's Merry Minstrels. Grapho and Jackson's Merry Minstrels.

Unscheduled entertainments would include the occasional shipwreck or beached whale. In the 1930s, the resort was so popular that you had to get to the beach not long after the crack of dawn to find a spare deck chair or even a grain of sand upon which to sit. Some of those born and raised under Queen Victoria, took the opportunity to lay down on the sand and get forty winks. Those wanting a bit of variety took a ride on a Seacar. This was a vehicle based on a Model T Ford with a boat-like chassis. It took passengers along the beach from Dundas Street, out into the water and onto the lifeboat slipway before returning along the Esplanade. All this was had for just a shilling (5p).

Swimwear fashions have changed over the years and the pretty lass in this photograph below, seems well aware of the stir she is causing with the men folk on this beach. Her modern, knitted two-piece was designed more to catch the eye than for practical purposes. Those who wore knitted costumes will remember with embarrassment how heavy and saggy they got when immersed in the sea. The first modern two-piece costume was created by Loius Reard in 1946, naming it the bikini after the atoll where atomic bomb tests were carried out. Reard reasoned that the costume's effects would be akin to that of a nuclear reaction and he was not far wrong.

Left: It was a quiet enough day as visitors to the front at Saltburn-by-the-Sea, in the last decade of the 19th century, enjoyed the lapping of the waters on the shore. Those brave enough to risk a dip in the North Sea were able to make use of the bathing machines that would protect the modesty of genteel ladies peeling off and slipping into the briny, without exposing their flesh to the gaze of all and sundry. The 500-yard-long pier opened in May 1869. It suffered damage from storms and wayward steamers over the years, but has somehow managed to survive thanks to various repairs and refurbishments. It is the last remaining pier in old Yorkshire.

Bottom left: This was a marvel of the age when installed in 1884. The Saltburn Cliff Lift is the oldest water balance machine of this type in the country. The arrival of the railway in the town in the early 1860s meant that tourism could be developed. However, access to the beach from the cliff top was nigh on suicidal. At first, a hoist was used, conveying 20 people at a time in a wooden cage. This was superseded by the funicular railway seen here that became as much an attraction as the pier and sands. The design was so efficient that little operational change has taken place in over 125 years.

Below: The sands at Marske have seen many interesting sights over the years. They have included smugglers of brandy, gin, rum, silks, tea, tobacco and other valuable items, much to the fury of the 'revenue men'. This storm-lashed coast also proved beneficial to locals beachcombing and 'liberating' goods washed up on the shoreline after a vessel had foundered in the dangerous North Sea breakers. In 1820, it was recorded that some 70 vessels went down between Marske and the Tees estuary in a single winter. In earlier times, this was a small, but fashionable, resort. A row of bathing huts was built at the foot of the sandbanks in the 1920s, replacing the old bathing machines. When not fishing, boat owners took visitors out for sea trips in the bay. The sands brought Malcolm Campbell here in 1922 to practise for an attempt on the world land speed record. He would be successful on Pendine Sands, in Wales, two years later.

TEESSIDE HORSE POWER

The cobbled setts are a delight to look at for those of us who like to look back to the 'good old days'. In reality, the road surface played havoc with one's sciatica as bicycle and cart wheels bumped along the road. The view is looking south with the nearby level crossing and Smeaton Street behind the camera. The toll bar in North Ormesby was not abolished until 31 July, 1916. Until then you dug deep and passed over a few coppers every time you passed this way. At this time, there were five such toll roads in Middlesbrough. They were done away with partly to help smooth the movement of materials needed for the war effort. The owners took a bit of persuading as the fees collected had been considerable. One proprietor, Lord Furness, received compensation that was the equivalent of over £250,000 in today's money. The large building on the right, with Nestles on the wall, was well known to locals as that of Greenwood's pawnbrokers.

Above, below and top right: Redcar's High Street begins at the junction with the Esplanade and provides a wide, airy entrance to the town's main shopping district. Lined with a variety of shops and houses in all shapes and sizes, the higgledy-piggledy way in which they come together is quaintly attractive. Unlike so many modern town centres, Redcar's retail experience is one that shouts of identity. Bland is a word we could use to describe many of Britain's shopping areas, but not that occupied by this special resort. The handsome drinking fountain once here was mainly used for quenching the thirst of horses, though no doubt riders enjoyed a refreshing draught from its bowl on occasions. The riders depicted were at the lower end of the road that is known more properly as High Street East. They were heading for the spot near the junction with

Queen Street where a clock tower in memory of King Edward VII would be erected, close to the National Provincial Bank building that opened in 1907. The

broad reaches of High Street narrow westward from Moore Street and the road is pedestrianised from here nowadays. The drinking fountain disappeared some years before the last war. Apparently, it came off second best in an argument with one of the motorcars that were seen more and more in the inter-war years as horses were consigned to the nostalgia banks. Another casualty of the passage of time is the lamplighter, seen going about his business on a ladder near Pearson's drapery.

Below: This 1940 motorist thought he had strayed into a different century, near Middlesbrough, when he encountered the Lowther State Coach in front of the Red Lion Hotel, on its way to its new home in Stewart Park. The outwardly attractive Austin 8 has slightly more horse power than the very elegant horse and carriage. The small saloon offered a reasonable standard of motoring for as little as £128 when it was launched at Longbridge, in 1939. Buying the new Austin Eight at the time, was advertised as 'An Outstanding Investment!'. The carriage on the other hand was not designed for the average man, but was in fact part of the lavish transport of the Lowther family, which had to be moved to a new home after Lowther Castle was closed in 1937. The state coach was used by the 5th Earl of Lonsdale who was noted for his extravagant spending.

Above: The former Middlesbrough Daimler Fleetline Northern Counties double decker looks quite a modern vehicle, even to our eyes in the second decade of the 21st century. Yet, the number plate gives away this lady's age as she must hail from the mid 1960s. It was en route from Seaton Carew to the outskirts of town, taking in a stretch of the journey unique to this part of the world. It used the Transporter Bridge to cross the river, something all locals take for granted. Yet, to visitors to Teesside this is something worthy of comment. For the rest of us it is commonplace. This model of bus was popular with passengers because of its easily accessed low floor.

Right: The Daimler buses were on the edge of Victoria Square on 28 March, 1973. They were part of the Fleetline group of vehicles first manufactured in 1961 as a low floored rival and equivalent to the Leyland Atlantean. By the end of the 1960s, the Daimler had become Middlesbrough's standard bus. Entering at the front of the vehicle was a whole new experience for passengers and it helped usher in the age of one-man operation. Central Library, the Police Station and the Law Courts can all be seen beyond

the roadway. The advert for Cavray's pies and sausages refers to Cavaghan and Gray, a Carlisle based company that was once that city's main employer. Cavray was one of the brand names it used.

Below: Traffic on Borough Road passes the ABC cinema in this December 1974 photograph. The mini van overtakes the ex-Saltburn Motor Services Bedford SB as it turns into Linthorpe Road. The coach was transferred to the Middlesbrough depot of Cleveland Transit for contract work and was also used on Seamer service No 27 for a time. The ABC was originally opened as the Elite Cinema in July 1923. It was modernised and renamed as the ABC in 1964. The interesting exterior with a monumental corner entrance has remained largely intact over the years. In the same year as this picture was taken the building interior was transformed into a triple cinema. Not many readers will remember the American B-movies showing on screen 3, but you may remember the fantastic atmosphere of the Saturday Morning ABC Minors. In 1974 the films that may have been screened were 'The Golden Voyage of Sinbad' and 'Flash Gordon'.

It might have been 16 December, 1974, but it is most unlikely that the transporter vehicle was bringing someone a Christmas present of these dimensions. Stockton High Street has seen some odd sights, but not many as jaw dropping as this one. Can you imagine trying to do a three point turn with this monster? Passengers on the top deck of the Daimler Fleetline bus belonging to Cleveland Transit craned their necks to get a better view. Although not completely certain, it is thought that the exceptional load was the stack for the Portland Incinerator.

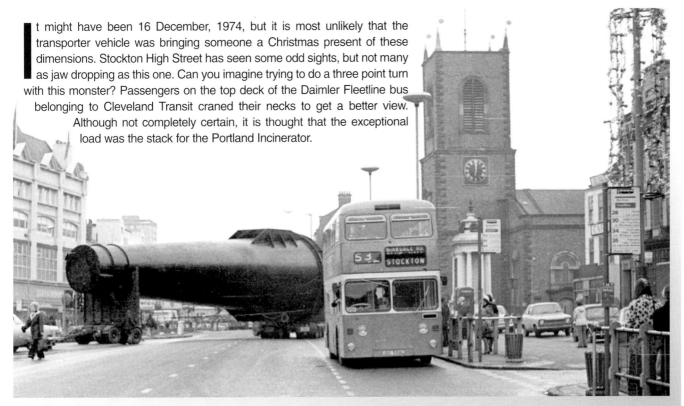

Two of these photographs were taken on 27 June, 1975, on Stockton High Street. The buses in main view were the former local Corporation's Leyland PD/2 Park Royal vehicles. In 1921, Stockton, Thornaby and Middlesbrough took charge of their own public transport needs by taking over the fleet and services previously handled by Imperial Tramways. Various makes of bus were used, with a strong push for Leylands taking place after the Second World War. The 58-seater passing the old Blackett's store was typical of the era. As time went by other models of Leylands were added, including those with Northern Counties or Weyman bodies. The other image was taken on Borough Road, Middlesbrough, on 19 August, 1972. The bus was a Guy Arab and ran on the Stockton to Eston route. Guy Motors was a Wolverhampton based firm and an important name in the world of motor transport from World War I until 1961 when it went bust. The name was kept alive by Jaguar and then BMC before British Leyland became involved. However, the factory was closed in 1982 and another famous name was no more. The slightly squashed appearance of this bus was deliberate. Known as a 'lowbridge' model, it had to negotiate a spot with restricted clearance on the route to and from the Transporter. The trio of long-haired guys hamming it up for the camera sported typical 70s' attire, with their flared trousers over platform shoes. Glam rock musicians helped popularise this footwear, sporting it on stage as they belted out 'Ballroom Blitz'.

WORK & INDUSTRY

This page: Newport Iron Works were situated not far from Newport Bridge on a site in between the river and railway. This was just one of many examples of heavy industry on Teesside and played an important role in Middlesbrough's growth. Particularly around the Cannon Street district, huge numbers of houses were jammed together to provide living accommodation for the families whose livelihood depended upon the foundries and their associated works.

Pollution being thrown out from the belching chimneys was a problem for clothes and lungs alike. This iron works was taken over by Dorman Long in 1917, but closed in 1930. The postcard picture of the Acklam plant (left) dates from 1907. By then, the company had

been acquired by the North Eastern Steel Company. It was set in what had once been a sleepy village, but all that changed in the scramble for iron and steel during the great shipbuilding and railway development of the second half of the 19th century. In the view across the river from Dock Point, there are two paddle powered tugs moored at the far bank. The timber yard belonging to the Middlesbrough Estate is to the right. The Estate could trace its history back to Norman times when tracts of land were given to monks in Whitby with the proviso that they maintained a chapel and its grounds in what was to become Middlesbrough. The Estate was bought by William Hustler in 1637 and stayed in family ownership for nearly 200 years. Joseph Pease and his partners bought the land in 1828 and modern Middlesbrough was born.

Above: Now that is a pretty sight to get any hot blooded male's temperature rising. There is something that little bit more exciting about a young woman's leg covered by policesheer nylon, rather than encased in tights or shapeless trousers. In April 1948, such stockings were still something of a prized possession. They had first been marketed in the USA at the end of the 1930s, so girls had to rely upon having a GI for a boyfriend in order to get their hands on a pair. Of course, nylon had other uses, such as material for parachutes and tents, so they only became widely available in shops after the war. Here, teenagers Joyce Meir and Lorraine Owens try on their fully fashioned hosiery given as a bonus to members of a workforce, probably at Foster, Clay and Ward at Cargo Fleet. Doreen Jones and Doreen Harrington selected underslips, but modesty stopped them from displaying anything else for the camera.

Middlesbrough College
Driving Ambition, Inspiring Success

In October 2012 renowned scientist Professor Lord Robert Winston officially opened the latest addition to the Middlesbrough education portfolio.

The leading education specialist, who presented the BBC's 'Child of Our Time' series, opened MC6, an A Level centre and Sports Academy at Middlesbrough College. The new building includes thirteen classrooms, tutorial and leisure facilities as well as four sports academies served by all-weather, multi-purpose pitches.

Middlesbrough College moved into brand new premise at the heart of Middlesbrough as part of the Middlehaven regeneration scheme in September 2008. The new premises proved so popular that within four years the College needed to expand and so built a new facility especially to accommodate its growing sixth-form provision.

The new building, whilst part of the modern regeneration of Middlesbrough, is located in an area that will have important memories for many local people as the area was once at the heart of Middlesbrough's industrial and commercial life. Whilst the college is very much focused on the present and future needs of local people, it also has an awareness of the heritage of the area and this is reflected in the building itself.

The building incorporates the carefully-preserved façade of one of the town's historic Victorian buildings – the Storrows Building, just one among many that was a part of a thriving industrial landscape around Middlesbrough Dock for over 140 years.

Top left: *The official opening ceremony: Left to right: Mike Hopkins, Principal, Professor Lord Robert Winston, Bob Brady OBE, Chairman of Governors, and Zoe Lewis, Deputy Principal.* **Below inset:** *The Storrows Building prior to incorporation into new College building.* **Bottom:** *New College building with Storrows Building visible.*

The Acklam Hall - the only Grade 1 listed building in Middlesbrough - was built in 1683 and for over 200 years was the home of the Hustler family. The family left the Hall in 1922 and in 1928 the Hall and grounds of 56 acres, including the tree-lined avenue and land almost to Ladgate Lane, were bought by Middlesbrough Corporation from Mostyn Hustler. The auctioneer's list suggests that no other bids were received: the sum offered by the Corporation was £11,500. A further £22,000 was spent on clearing outbuildings, adapting, extending and furnishing and equipping the property to enable it to open as a school.

Acklam Hall Secondary School opened in 1935 with 231 pupils. However, the school soon outgrew its accommodation.

Although we do not know who the architect of the building was, we do know it was built around 1860, some 16 years after the Middlesbrough Dock came into existence. It was one of many engineering works that came into existence during the rapid industrial expansion of Middlesbrough in the second half of the nineteenth century.

Between 1951 and 1958 the remaining ornamental gardens were removed and extensions built for Acklam Hall Grammar School, at a cost of £82,046.

Situated as it was, close to the busy Middlesbrough Dock, the premises later became the premises of J W Storrow & Co. who were ship chandlers and sail-makers.

The extensions comprised a two-storey teaching block with attached single-storey practical rooms, linked to the old building to the east by a new assembly hall with stage and entrance vestibule. The new wing had on the ground floor two classrooms, two art and crafts rooms, two woodwork rooms, and on the first floor five classrooms, access to which was provided by two staircases. A corridor running behind the stage gave access to the ground floor teaching rooms which were readily available for use as 'green rooms'.

It is perhaps hard for the young people studying at the College today to appreciate but many of the ships that berthed in the dock relied on sails to power them on their trade routes and a sail-maker would be an important part of life in the dock. As late as 1911 the three-masted sailing ship 'Caradoc' was berthed in Middlesbrough Dock.

*Top: Acklam Hall in 1938. **Centre and below:** The extension of Acklam Hall in progress (centre) and completed (below), 1958.*

The Storrows Building itself was a two-storey, red-brick stucture whose design included some delicate and attractive features that perhaps one would not expect to find in a property built with such a utilitarian purpose. The elevation facing onto Dock Street has curved heads to the windows and doors with a bull-eye feature in the gable, as well as attractive brick pilasters and corbelling. It is this façade that is now part of the new College building.

The recent expansion of the college is just the latest example of something that has happened regularly over the decades as new buildings are created to cope with expanding student numbers.

The present Middlesbrough College was created when the College relocated in September 2008 from its four previous sites - at Acklam, Longlands, Kirby and Marton.

The sixth form of the new Acklam High School was provided with its own accommodation by 1971 as the last flower beds of the Hall were removed. At the same time a new House Block was constructed incorporating six house rooms, associated teaching spaces and ancillary accommodation. There was also a new sports hall and a swimming pool.

In 1974, Acklam High School split to form Kings Manor 11-16 School and Acklam Sixth Form College, each occupying one of two new teaching blocks in front of the original manor house, within which accommodation was shared.

The Kings Manor building suffered the fate of being destroyed by fire following which Kings Manor School moved across Hall Drive to the site shared with Hall Garth School. The block was finally demolished in 1997 leaving Acklam Sixth Form College as the sole occupant of the site.

The assembly hall with a floor area of 3,150 sq ft had a fully-equipped stage with storage below, and opened onto a new vestibule entrance which would now constitute the main entrance to the school through which access could be gained to the old building. At the time it was wryly noted that that 'attic bedrooms can have their disadvantages when used as classrooms.'

These new extensions enabled the school to accommodate 540 pupils, including 90 in the sixth form.

Further expansion prompted more developments in subsequent years.

In 1967, Acklam Hall Grammar School for Boys became the 13-18 non-selective Acklam High School and also became co-educational by amalgamating with Kirby Girls Grammar School, which was then closed.

Acklam Sixth Form College merged with Kirby College and subsequently became part of Middlesbrough College.

The Longlands College came about in September 1959 as a direct consequence of the growth in student numbers at Constantine College of Technology.

Constantine College had been opened on 16 September, 1929, with just 36 full-time, 48 part-time and 1,220 evening students. By 1949 it had 325 full-time and 1,096 part-time students as well as more than 2,000 evening students.

Top left: *The official opening programme of Acklam High School extensions, 1971.* **Left and above:** *New additions to Acklam High School in 1971; a sixth form Common Room (left) and Swimming Pool (above).*

It had out-grown its accommodation and was also looking to transform itself into an institution of higher education, a process which over the subsequent decades would see it transform first into Teesside Polytechnic and then into the present-day Teesside University.

Decentralisation began in 1954 with the administrative and physical removal of Art courses from Constantine College (although the permanent College of Art building did not open until 1958). Pressure of numbers saw the use of large amounts of temporary accommodation in various parts of Middlesbrough, and it was a relief when in September 1958 Longlands College, on Douglas Street, opened as an annexe.

The administrative separation of Longlands College from its parent took place in September 1959, on the basis that Longlands would provide less advanced courses, with priority being given to engineering. In subsequent years the college would offer courses relevant to many of the local industries: chemical plant operation, pattern making and foundry technology, electrical installation, instrumentation, telecommunications, motor vehicle mechanics, naval architecture, metallurgy and plumbing. However, the early Longlands College offered a much wider range of courses: under Principal Mr J Wood the College also offered courses in hairdressing, horticulture, bread making, cake decoration, and even courses for those wishing to train as dental technicians.

Once again a growth in demand meant that there was a need for additional accommodation.

County Borough of Teesside

Extensions to Longlands College

OFFICIAL OPENING

Wednesday 27th November 1968

On 27 November, 1968, Shirley Williams MP, Minister of State for the Department of Education and Science, officially opened extensions to Longlands College of Further Education. The extensions, which cost nearly £700,000, doubled the area of the buildings and included a new four-storey wing, workshops and a sports hall.

Additional class and laboratory provision was located in the new wing linked to the existing four-storey block to create extensions to departments which, with the sports hall, communal and administrative accommodation, had been formed around a courtyard served at each corner by a staircase. Additional workshops were formed by double banking with the existing workshop block and extending a U-shaped wing around the service road.

From September 1965 Longlands College was joined by another further education provider: Kirby College of Further Education.

COUNTY BOROUGH OF TEESSIDE
EDUCATION COMMITTEE

Official Opening
of
Extensions to Longlands College
of Further Education
by
MRS. SHIRLEY WILLIAMS, M.P.
(Minister of State, Department of Education and Science)

WEDNESDAY 27th NOVEMBER 1968 at 10-45 a.m.

Top left and top right: The Domestic Science room (top left) and Library at Acklam High School after the 1971 extensions. *Left and above:* Programmes from the official opening of Extensions to Longlands College in 1968.

The Department of Education and Science agreed with a proposal to demolish the original block and replace it with a much larger two-storey building. The new block would house the food and fashion departments and be linked to the main building and the drama block at both ground and first floors.

Additionally, a new main entrance to the College was formed on the ground floor as a link between the old building and the new. The ground floor of the drama block was extended to provide extra cloakroom facilities adjacent to the students' common room.

A new wing including specialist catering, hairdressing, and office-practice facilities, as well as improved library and communal facilities was officially opened in September 1972 by Lord Boyle of Handsworth. At this time the Principal was Mr G J Edwards and the College accommodated 520 full-time, and 5,000 part-time, students.

The Kirby College of Further Education was originally established in September 1965 as the West Middlesbrough College of Further Education. The nucleus of the new college had been created by the transfer from Constantine College of Technology of commercial, secretarial and GCE courses. In 1966, the College assumed responsibility for courses in breadmaking hairdressing, pre-nursing and horticulture, which had previously been offered at the Longlands College of Further Education. In 1967, the Women's Educational Centre, based in The Barns building on Orchard Road, became the Department of Food and Fashion and was integrated into the College.

THE RT. HON. LORD BOYLE OF HANDSWORTH,
M.A., D.Sc., LL.D.

COUNTY BOROUGH OF TEESSIDE
EDUCATION COMMITTEE

Official Opening
of
KIRBY COLLEGE OF FURTHER EDUCATION
EXTENSIONS
by
The Rt. Hon. Lord Boyle of Handsworth,
M.A., D.Sc., LL.D.
Vice-Chancellor of the University of Leeds

Wednesday, 20th September, 1972
at 3-00 p.m.

Marton Sixth Form College was established on Marton Road in what had formerly been the premises of Middlesbrough High School.

Middlesbrough High School for Boys had been established in 1870 in Grange Road. A High School for Girls was opened in 1874. Both schools transferred to new buildings on King Edwards Road in 1877.

*Top left and Below: New facilities at Kirby College after the 1972 extension included a Retail Trade Room (top left) and Student Concourse (below). **Above and top, facing page:** Official opening programmes of the Kirby College of Further Education extensions in 1972.*

The College was originally housed in the former Middlesbrough Girls High School building in King Edwards Road and in an annexe in Marton Grove. However, it was always the intention that the College would occupy the premises vacated by Kirby Girls Grammar School on Roman Road. From 1966 onwards the premises at Roman Road were extended to include a five-storey teaching block and a two storey communal block. In 1968 the premises were occupied by Kirby College of Further Education.

The pre-war single-storey classroom block facing Roman Road was, however, considered to be unsuitable for satisfactory alterations to meet the needs of the new College.

Extensions to Constantine College of Technology and recognition that Victorian buildings were inappropriate for 20th century education prompted relocation in 1959 to new premises on Marton Road, which in 1974 became the base for Marton Sixth Form College.

During the latter part of the 20th century there were a number of mergers of further education and sixth-form colleges and the present Middlesbrough College came into being on 1 August, 2002.

Ironically, although Middlesbrough College moved to its present location from four sites spread around the town, it has moved to a place closer to the historical orgins of adult education in the town as the first opportunity for adults in Middlesbrough to pursue educational courses was provided from premises that were within a few streets of the present college location.

Middlesbrough as the 'Infant Hercules' was founded on industries that required considerable technical and scientific knowledge and skills.

The Ironmasters came from Germany, Wales, Staffordshire and East Anglia and brought the men with these skills to the place where they could be harnessed to the raw materials of coal and iron. There was a need, however, to train and educate local people if growth was to be sustained.

In 1844, the Middlesbrough Mechanics Institute was established in West Street. Funding was provided by Henry Bolckow, John Vaughan and Isaac Wilson and the Institute had 104 members.

The purpose of the Institute was 'to provide for the diffusion of useful knowledge among the working classes, by the establishment of a library and reading room, occasional lectures on subjects of general information and by instruction in the practical branches of science'.

There were early difficulties, not least the reluctance of employers to release workers, and the Institute almost collapsed in 1857.

However, by 1860 the Mechanics Institute was able to move into larger premises in Durham Street, also a short distance from the present college. In doing so it acquired laboratories, enabling it to offer lectures on chemistry: in the eight months between

KIRBY COLLEGE OF FURTHER EDUCATION—EXTENSIONS

OFFICIAL OPENING

WEDNESDAY, 20th SEPTEMBER, 1972

COUNTY BOROUGH OF TEESSIDE

October 1862 and May 1863 there were 29 lectures on Inorganic Chemistry, some of which were open to the public.

By 1870, the Mechanics Institute offered an Art school with daytime classes and the following year there were Evening classes in Maths, Technical Drawing and Architectural Drawing. However, there were still problems with recruiting students and it was suggested that the location was too far from the growing urban sprawl to the south of the town. The Mechanics Institute struggled and finally closed its doors in 1896.

However, the seeds of post-school education had been sown and this in due course led to the present day Middlesbrough College which provides a wide range of educational opportunities for over 10,000 students in the first decade of the twenty-first century.

Below: The Mechanics Institute which moved to new premises in Durham Street 1860.

INEOS Nitriles

Seal Sands on Teesside is a name long associated with the chemical industry. Today there are over 10 companies that make this area one of the largest chemical sites in Europe. One of those companies is INEOS Nitriles who, with four global manufacturing sites, produce and supply the world with acrylonitrile.

Acrylonitrile-based acrylic fibres are a popular substitute for cotton and wool and are used to make clothing, carpeting and blankets. Derivatives for Acrylonitrile produce ABS plastic increasingly used in automotive and technology markets, in rubber, or as solvents in the production of insulin and antibiotics.

As the core ingredient needed to make carbon fibre, it has revolutionised materials technology from the extraordinary artificial limbs worn by paralympian sprinters at the London 2012 Paralympic Games, to modern aircraft, motor racing and space exploration.

Left: The Mayor of Middlesbrough, Alderman Jack Brown, cutting the tape at the opening ceremony of the site on 10 September, 1968, on his left is Plant Manager Norman Roberts. Below: Looking east in 1968 over the Monsanto Greenfield site prior to construction of a new Acrylonitrile plant. Below inset: Acrylonitrile 4 column being delivered by sea.

sandbanks at Seal Sands, but by 1930 dredging and pollution resulted in a dramatic decline in their population and until recently seals were rarely seen. A reversal has occured since the 1960s so that now grey and common seals come to bask and calve.

The Industry Nature Conversation Association (INCA) acquired a large area of the mud flats for a National Nature Reserve, which is a site of special Scientific Interest and a Site of International Importance for water birds.

Yet the piece of land where this magic of chemistry occurs is of international significance not only because of its industry. Seal Sands has always been of importance as it is the only area of inter-tidal mud flats between Holy Island to the north and the Humber estuary to the south. The mud flats at Seal Sands have evolved as sedimentation has collected following the decreased energy of the River Tees as it reaches its mouth, thus making it rich in organic content and hence particularly attractive to wildlife.

Despite the extensive local industry the sands provide a sense of isolation even though it is flanked by dense urban areas such a Hartlepool and Billingham.

As a result, the area can see up to 30,000 ducks and waders in the autumn and winter months. They in turn attract raptors such as peregrine falcons and short-eared owls which use the industrial infrastructure as perches and nesting sites.

Surprisingly, the industrial lighting actually helps wading birds to feed around the clock.

Not to forget the wildlife that gave Seal Sands its name. More than a 1,000 seals lounged on the

Top left: Completion of the first plant, Acrylonitrile, the second plant to be built on the mud flats. ***Below:*** Steam locomotive 62005. Withdrawn from service by British Railways in December 1967, it was hired in 1968 to provide steam to the AN4 plant. ***Above:*** Site expansion in 1977 with the building of six warehouses which came from London Docks. Each warehouse was dismantled by Lumus who numbered each part before they were shipped to Seal Sands to be erected on site piece by piece.

This development at Seal Sands has shown that the chemical industry and nature conservation can coexist. Today, reed beds ingest unwanted organic residues and technical developments continue to reduce emissions to negligible levels.

Industry has been in the area since the Romans panned for salt at Greatham, where salt is still extracted today. During the Great War of 1914-1918 the British chemical industry received a huge boost from the demand for munitions. Locally this meant synthetic ammonia for use in explosives was produced in vast quantities at Billingham. Dorman Long, founders of the famous Teesside Steelworks, was established in 1917; this heritage together with coal and ship building provided Teesside with the skills needed for the successful development of a chemical industry that today produces sodium chlorine, Polyethylene and Nylon.

Above: Expansion of the site with the replacement of A N 4 with a larger AN 6 plant, a downstream Adiponitirle process and HMD plant, a utilities plant for steam, an energy and an effluent plant to deal with waste, offices, laboratories, a canteen and a fire station. **Left:** *With over 1,000 people on site, sports and social events were well supported with golf, 5-a-side football, badminton and squash. Pictured are members of the inter-department 5-a-side football teams of 1981.*

The same decade saw Monsanto expand acrylonitrile production in the area, which was a great boost to the local economy. The company wanted to recruit and train its own personnel from all aspects of society and were particularly keen to employ those with work ethics such as former policemen and military personnel. The first Process Operators included life guards, door-to-door salesmen, teachers, fitters and mechanics.

Over 1,000 hectares of Seal Sands were reclaimed in 1955 and by 1966 a Philips Imperial Petroleum (Conoco Philips) refinery and the Monsanto (INEOS) Acrylics plant were built. The lack of infrastructure demanded innovative thinking. River and rail connections were used to bring in the larger equipment needed, but the power to build and run the plants was provided by a locomotive that was no longer required by British Rail. In the 1970s, the opening of the Seal Sands Road connected the area to the A19 and encouraged further progress. One of the most extraordinary developments at Seal Sands took place under the sea with a 220-mile-long pipeline operated by Conoco Phillips which runs from Teesside to the ECOFYSK oil and gas platforms in the North Sea,

Top and above: The company took science into primary schools with the support of David Bellamy (author, broadcaster, environmental campaigner and botanist, pictured top left) and introduced the world of work to Grangefield School. *Below:* The 1990s saw further expansion to the site with a new Research and Development building, a CoGeneration plant and a gasification plant.

The site changed hands in 1985 when it was bought by BASF, Further expansion enabled it to produce its own energy and export to the national grid. In 2008, the site changed hands again when it was acquired by INEOS Nitriles as BASF moved out of bulk chemicals.

The INEOS Group is one of the top chemical companies in the world and the second largest private company in the United Kingdom. Formed in 1998 as a management buyout of former BP petrochemical assets in Belgium, it has since expanded by acquiring several business and assets from BP, BASF, ICI, Dow, Solvay, Degussa and UCB. Further acquisitions and joint ventures have resulted in a group of companies with a turnover in excess of $43 billion

With the acquisition of BP chemicals in 2005 INEOS Nitriles was formed; a global business that provides 95% of the world's acrylonitrile technology and production. The acquisition of the Seal Sands site in 2008 brought with it new focus, which rejuvenated the business.

INEOS showed an increased emphasis on both safety and innovation which resulted in updated plant, new equipment and control systems.

Top: *Following the purchase of the site by INEOS Nitriles in 2008, the plants were updated with new pipe and up-to-date equipment and control systems.* **Left:** *Forging new links within the community with the site fire brigade now run by the Cleveland County Fire Brigade.*

INEOS implemented a formal and rigorous training programme focused on process and safety which has been recognised by the Cogent Gold Standard award. New links have been forged with the community, such as those with the Cleveland County Fire Brigade which is to provide the on-site emergency services. To address an aging workforce and recruiting needs the INEOS apprentice programme has being expanded to provide work experience for engineering students and those wishing to establish a career in the industry. Today, the site provides direct employment for nearly 400 people and supports indirectly over 1,000 jobs in the area.

INEOS Nitriles at Seal Sands is delighted to be part of the INEOS Group, which is a dynamic international organisation. It is equally proud of its role in Teesside's industry and the local community. As the current owner of the site the company is proud of its part in a long and distinguished heritage reflecting the traditions of Teesside.

Above: Fire training at Durham Tees Valley Airport. **Below:** *A bird's eye view of the Seal Sands site, 2012.*

Svitzer Marine
Seahorses and Salvage

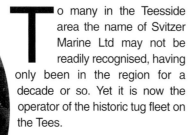

To many in the Teesside area the name of Svitzer Marine Ltd may not be readily recognised, having only been in the region for a decade or so. Yet it is now the operator of the historic tug fleet on the Tees.

With headquarters in Copenhagen, the Group has regional offices in Amsterdam, Cape Town, Dubai, Gothenburg, Miami, Sydney, Singapore and Middlesbrough, and three divisional offices: Esvagt in Esbjerg, Ocean Towage in Amsterdam and Salvage in Ijmuiden. Svitzer's harbour towage activities cover some 80 ports in 13 countries.

But the thought of tugs will always bring back the name of the original firm, the Tees Towing Company.

The Tees Towing Company traced its origin on the river back to 1920, when the Robinson Tug Company Limited amalgamated with the Tees Tug Company Limited. In essence the current port operation is the direct descendant nearly a century on.

When first formed the company was operating a fleet of some 20 vessels, mainly powered by steam. These were acquired via the amalgamation of several smaller companies from 1880 through to 1918. The main founder of the company was William Henry Crosthwaite (1880-1968).

William Crosthwaite was born in Elder Street, Middlesbrough, and in his youth went to sea. It was in 1904 that he took his first step into 'tugownery' when, with partners James Blumer and John Graham, he bought the iron screw tug Primrose from the Florence Tugboat & Salvage Co. The purchase was soon followed by the acquisition of the paddle tug Challenger. How 24 year old Crosthwaite raised the funds for these ventures is something of a mystery, but by 1906 he had become the largest shareholder in the Florence company, with its offices at 7, Dock Street.

When Crosthwaite acquired the Florence company he also acquired its tug Florence with a seahorse symbol on its paddle boxes and the motto 'Facta non verba' – 'Deeds not words'. The motto and symbol would remain part of the Tees Towing Company long after the Florence was history.

Crosthwaite founded the Tees Tug Company in 1909.

The Tees Tug Company, Ltd.
IN WHICH IS INCORPORATED
WATKINS PETRIE, LIMITED.

W. H. CROSTHWAITE — Managing Director.

Owners of the Largest, most Powerful and best equipped Fleet of Tugs on the North-East Coast.

SCREW TUGS:
Empress of India, Liberia, Glen Rosa, Vixen, Knight of St. George, Primrose, Clarissa, Hero.

DOUBLE-ENGINED PADDLE TUGS:
Challenger, Champion, Florence, Triumph, Hibernia, Scotia.

National Telephone (all hours) - No. 357.
Telegraphic Address - "Tug, Middlesbrough."

15 DOCK STREET, MIDDLESBRO'.

Top left: Sir William Henry Crosthwaite founder of the Tees Towing Company wearing his mayoral robes and chain of office in 1925. Above: A Tees Tug Company advertisement from 1913 indicating the absorption of the Watkins Petrie Company. Below: The Florence in Middlesbrough Dock Cut in 1926.

The Tees Towing Company was formed in 1920 to acquire the assets of the Tees Tug Company and the Robinson Tug Company, a merger which Crosthwaite had long been working towards. The new company boasted no fewer than 15 tugs and was valued at over £55,000. Four more vessels were owned by the associated company Charles Duncan & Sons.

Crosthwaite really was a local lad made good and in 1925 he became the 67th Mayor of Middlesbrough.

Hard times, however, lay ahead.

By the end of 1930 the combined fleet of vessels owned by Tees Towing, and the now associated firms of Charles Duncan, Middlesbrough Towage and the Crosthwaite Steamship company, comprised 12 vessels with an average age of 35 years; a very high figure. And by 1932, four of the eight tugs were laid up and the crews were out of work.

William Crosthwaite was knighted in the New Year Honours' list of 1939 and later that same year he became Mayor of Middlesbrough once again but with a war about to start, however, there would be more hard times ahead.

During the early part of the Second World War three of the Tees Towing fleet were requisitioned by the Ministry of Shipping.

Inevitably, salvage work soon began arriving for the remaining fleet. The first such work came on 27 September 1940, when the minesweeper HMS Halcyon hit a mine shortly after leaving the mouth of the Tees. The tug Acklam Cross went to the rescue. The episode was just the first of 24 that year.

All through the six years of war Tees Towing and Duncan tugs were heavily occupied in dealing with vessels of the Royal and Allied navies, from large destroyers to the largest landing craft which were either newly built or in the river for repair or replenishment. Many types of landing craft were built at Stockton, Haverton Hill, Middlesbrough and South Bank. In total some 60 ships and almost 300 large landing craft were built on the river during the war.

In 1944, components for the Mulberry Harbours, the floating docks needed in the invasion of Normandy were built in many locations around Britain, including the Tees.

Top: *The Berlin is assisted into dock by Athlete and George Robinson. At the time, around 1920, it was the largest vessel to have visited Middlesbrough Dock.* ***Above:*** *Robinson & Crosthwaite advertising from 1930.*

Two of the concrete caissons code named Phoenix were built in the Graythorp dry dock of William Gray, and would be handled out of the building dock by local tugs such as the Acklam Cross and Cleveland before being taken south. It later fell to tugs Euston Cross and Charing Cross to join the armada taking the harbours across the English Channel to France.

In the First World War the company had lost two vessels. Happily, it survived the Second World War with no losses. Tragically, however, in peacetime, in 1946 five crew members were lost in the Tees itself when the tug George Robinson towing the steamer SS Imperial Valley sank after the steamer and the tug collided.

By 1949, over 4,000 ships cleared the river, yet in the following years numbers began to decline. Salvage jobs meanwhile averaged eight or so per year. The 1950s would be years of consolidation, and innovation.

William Henry Crosthwaite died in 1968. During 1977 Richard Crosthwaite was appointed joint Managing Director of Tees Towing Co Ltd, sharing the position with his father Cecil Crosthwaite, but beginning to take over the lead in managing the company.

Major Cecil Crosthwaite, Lord Lieutenant of Cleveland, died on Christmas Day 1978. Ever since his return home from the war he had worked alongside his father, Sir William, in the modernisation of the tug fleet.

Richard Crosthwaite now became Chairman and Managing Director.

Early in 1983 a decision was made to replace the riverside headquarters with a new purpose-built building slightly to the west of the existing structure. The old buildings, partly timber, had been in use since 1952. Five acres of adjacent land were acquired from George Cohen Sons & Co Ltd. The new HQ opened in 1984.

In late 1990, following the earlier untimely death of Richard Crosthwaite, the Tees Towing Company was sold to Cory Towage Ltd., a subsidiary of the Ocean Group with a long maritime background. Under Cory Towage, the company continued to invest in the Tees with further additions to the fleet, the Fiery Cross and Phoenix Cross, two fire-fighting tugs were added to it. The decision to enhance the fleet with new fire-fighting tugs was partly as a result of the SKL1 ferry incident off Saltburn when the vessel took fire and ultimately sank following an onboard explosion - this after the crews had valiantly tried to save the vessel and tow it into port in appalling weather.

A further enhancement to the fleet was made just as Ocean Group sold Cory Towage to the Dutch Wijsmuller Group in 2000 with the arrival of the new Ayton Cross and Ormesby Cross. Reflecting the changes in the UK shipbuilding industry these two vessels were built overseas in Spain, a first for the Tees to have 'imported' tugs.

In 2001, the whole group was taken over by Svitzer, a division of the giant Maersk Group.

Svitzer's story begins in 1833 when Emil Zeuthen Svitzer was 27 years old. At the age of 14 he secured a traineeship in a trading company in Copenhagen whose business included shipbuilding.

Top: Cecil Crosthwaite (left) and Richard Crosthwaite (right). *Below:* The Tees Towing fleet in 1965. *Above:* Emil Zeuthen Svitzer.

In 1829 Svitzer gained his trade licence and became a partner in the timber trading company J.A. Lange & Co. When Lange died Svitzer took over.

Timber was mainly shipped to Copenhagen from Norway and Sweden and some of Svitzer's shipments were wrecked. This gave birth to the idea of starting a salvage company.

Recognising that he was a tradesman, not a sailor, Svitzer partnered with master mariner H.C. Larsen. Practical knowledge of seamanship and relationships within the shipping industry were crucial to succeed in salvage.

The first vessels in the Svitzer fleet were a broad flat-bottomed cutter, Gammelholm, bought from the Danish navy, a sprit-sail rigged boat and a large gig.

The terms of a salvage contract were negotiated between the captain of the ship and the salvage master. It was therefore crucial for the salvage company to be at the right location at the right time and for the salvage master to be able to make a quick and realistic assessment of the job. This included estimating the value of the vessel and cargo and, of course, the work, equipment and manpower required to get the vessel safely to port.

Svitzer acquired Denmark's first diving equipment in 1842. This quickly became important salvage gear.

The cutter Nancy, bought in 1853, was stationed in Frederikshavn in north-east Jutland and assisted vessels in the Kattegat, where there was a steady trade between Jutland and Norway.

Left: A model of the Gammelholm, the first salvage vessel in the Svitzer fleet. Above: Svitzer acquired Denmark's first diving equipment in 1842. This quickly became important salvage gear. Below: Photo of the Svitzer diver J. Danielsen taken in 1895 when divers examined and repaired International of Newcastle. He is ready for a dive on board the salvage vessel Hertha, built by Svitzer in 1877. The diving helmet was connected to an air hose through which the crew on board a vessel could pump air to the diver. The divers used gas lamps underwater when inspecting and working on the wrecks.

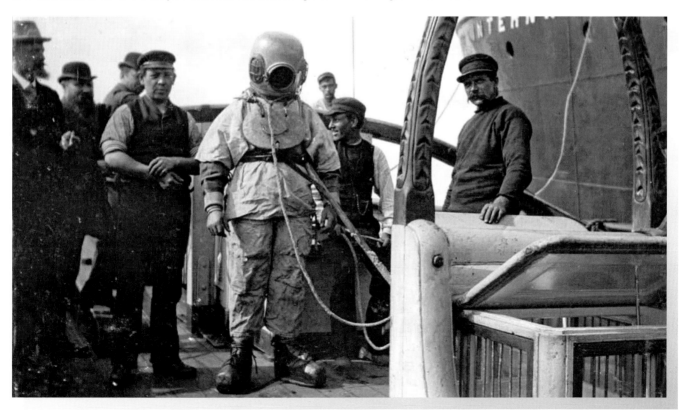

The need for more pulling power was imperative for the salvage company to undertake bigger operations. In 1860 Svitzer salvaged a steamer which had sunk to the bottom of the Swedish Lake Väneren. Svitzer recovered the steamer using seven sailing vessels and two pontoons. The wreck was later bought by Svitzer, rebuilt as a specialist salvage vessel and renamed Skandinavien. With an engine power of 55 hp it was a powerful vessel at the time.

The development of the steam engine, however, soon presented another challenge. Steam tug boats started to emerge strong enough to pull grounded but otherwise undamaged vessels free without using special equipment or expertise – often at a more competitive price than a specialised salvage company. The introduction of ballasting systems too intensified this trend as grounded vessels were often able to re-float merely with the aid of pulling power and deballasting.

On 1 January 1872, the entire salvage equipment of Svitzer was sold to the limited company Em. Z. Svitzers Bjergningsentreprise. Em. Z. Svitzer himself had seven shares; his staff had 26 and the board 11, in total 44 shares giving them the majority interest in the company. Svitzer remained the managing director.

The capital raised was used for new equipment and four salvage vessels.

Hans Peter Johan Lyngbye took over the management of the company in 1886 upon Emil Svitzer's death.

In 1889 the steamship Em. Z. Svitzer arrived in Marseilles to undertake salvage operations in the Mediterranean. In a similar alliance in 1906 the salvage vessel Protector was stationed as far away as China.

Only one vessel was lost during the First World War. The salvage vessel Danmark, stationed in Constantinople, was confiscated by the Turkish government in 1915. The vessel was never returned to Svitzer but later used to compete against its former owner.

During the Second World War, Svitzer's salvage operations largely continued during the German occupation of Denmark. Many vessels in distress needed assistance owing to damage caused by mines. Svitzer had ten salvage vessels and two lifting pontoons at work in Danish waters. Several Svitzer vessels were damaged by mines, but only one was lost, tragically with the entire crew of seven.

When war broke out Svitzer had five vessels stationed abroad.

Top: The French steamer Atlantique grounded and later rescued by the salvage vessel EM. Z. Svitzer – the company's first vessel stationed in the Mediterranean. **Above:** In 1940 Svitzer purchased 10 underwater cutting machines allowing divers to work with a blowtorch below water. **Left:** A Svitzer salvage operation in progress.

All were used by allied forces. Protector, stationed in the Red Sea, was quickly put to work for the allies. Valkyrien was in Lisbon at the time of the German occupation of Denmark; her Captain decided to leave the harbour and surrender her voluntarily to the British.

In order to avoid subsequent German confiscation of Svitzer vessels, an escape to Sweden was planned with the Danish Resistance. Svitzer's vessels sailed into Swedish waters on 9 April, 1945, exactly five years from the day Germany occupied Denmark.

Post-war, the international recognition gained from years of working abroad resulted in a high profile contract in 1956. Svitzer, together with the Dutch salvage company L. Smit & Co's Internationale Sleepdienst, was appointed by the United Nations to clear the Suez Canal of wrecks following the Suez crisis.

Since 1979 Svitzer has been a part of the A.P. Moller-Maersk Group.

In 1999, Svitzer became a regional towage operator when it acquired the Swedish towage company Röda Bolaget. The acquisition of Wijsmuller in 2001 added harbour and terminal towage operations around the world.

Back in 1833 Emil Svitzer began his salvage business with a careful blend of well suited vessels, skilful employees, comprehensive relationships and information networks, cooperating with the local communities and operating from strategically important locations.

Since then the company has overcome tough competitive circumstances, economic recessions, world crises and fundamental technological and market changes.

More than 4,000 Svitzer employees now operate some 500 vessels in more than 35 countries.

Svitzer commitment to the Tees has been emphasised by the renewing of its Tees fleet with the arrival of the Svitzer Hutton in 2011, and the Svitzer Castle in 2012.

*Top: Icons of the Tees: Svitzer's Ormesby Cross, Coatham Cross, Phoenix Cross and Ayton Cross pictured with the world famous Tees Transporter Bridge in the background. **Above left:** Svitzer Bootle assists the Laura to dock. **Below:** Svitzer Marine's Tees Wharf premises.*

Sahaviriya Steel Industries
The Rebirth of Steelmaking

Thanks to Sahaviriya Steel Industries Public Company Limited (SSI), iron and steel making has returned to Teesside after a two year absence.

The iron and steel story in the area, however, begins nearly two centuries ago.

The planned town of Middlesbrough, begun in 1830, was developed by a group of Quaker businessmen who held interests in South Durham coal mines and the Stockton and Darlington railway.

In 1839, Henry Bolckow and John Vaughan set up an iron and engineering works in the new town, employing Scots pig iron and Durham coke to make iron products for the marine and agricultural engineering trades. The partners established their own blast furnaces at Witton Park, in County Durham.

Following a two years search for iron ore, Vaughan and the mining engineer, John Marley, identified the 16 ft 'Main Seam' at Upleatham in the Eston Hills. For the next 25 years it served to make Middlesbrough the iron making capital of the world.

Top: The rebirth of steelmaking on Teesside, the blast furnace by night, 2012. Left: A 19th century indenture, the legal foundation of iron and steel prosperity. Above: 19th century accounting ledgers from Bell Bros., part of the British Steel Collection at Teesside Archives.

Bolckow and Vaughan built their first Cleveland blast furnaces at Eston and Middlesbrough in 1852. Over the next 20 years blast furnaces appeared along the south side of the Tees from Stockton and Thornaby, through west and east Middlesbrough to Cargo Fleet, Eston and South Bank with outposts in Lackenby and Redcar. Bell Bros. developed a site north of the river.

At the peak of pig iron production there were almost 120 blast furnaces on the Tees. By 1860 production was 500,000 tons: in the boom year of 1873 it topped two million tons.

The number of Teesside puddling furnaces (where pig iron was converted to malleable wrought iron) rose from under 200 in 1863 to 750 ten years later. At the height of the boom the district produced 600,000 tons of wrought iron annually.

By the end of the 1870s, however, steel had replaced iron almost entirely in the rail market and was beginning to challenge for the ship plate and boiler trade.

In the early 1870s, Bolckow Vaughan acquired a steel works in Manchester and interests in Spanish iron mines. By the end of the decade the company was producing 'acid steel' by the Bessemer process. But it was also actively pursuing the means to use Cleveland ores, and in 1879 the new Thomas-Gilchrist method used a base material (limestone or dolomite) to line the converter, giving it the name 'basic steel' production.

Steel making was driven by the new firm of Dorman Long, established in Middlesbrough in 1875. A J Dorman and Albert de Lande Long bought West Marsh to make iron bars and angles for shipbuilding. They acquired Samuelson's Britannia Works in 1882. Dorman Long was producing 100,000 tons of steel a year by 1890. As a result of experiments to make open hearth steel using Cleveland ores, Dorman Long began to work closely with Bell Brothers of Port Clarence and in 1899 the firms merged. This was supplemented by the acquisition of the North Eastern Steel Company along with the Ayrton sheet mills and the Cleveland wire mills. By 1904 Dorman Long was producing 450,000 tons of steel.

Meanwhile, Bolckow Vaughan had developed steel production using the Basic Bessemer system at their huge Eston works and the South Durham Steel and Iron Company.

The South Durham Company was a venture launched by Hartlepool shipping tycoon Sir Christopher Furness. In the early 1900s, he acquired the Cargo Fleet Iron Company whose modern, integrated site quickly challenged the dominance of Dorman Long and Bolckow Vaughan, producing around 125,000 tons of coke, pig iron and steel a year. By 1914, the many firms which had dominated the Cleveland iron trade had been reduced to three giants.

Top left: A group of workmen c.1900. **Above:** *Ironstone miner leading his pony to the surface, c. 1927.* **Below:** *Dixon's Dockyard 1921. Note Middlesbrough Ironworks to the right and Port Clarence in the foreground.*

Demand for iron and steel for the war effort bolstered the industry. Of particular significance was the acquisition by Dorman Long of Walker's works at Redcar in 1915, as well as the Newport works in Middlesbrough two years later. It further extended production by converting the North Eastern Steel Company's works to open hearth production from 1919.

By the end of 1920, however, the industry was suffering. The big three firms tried to protect themselves by acquisitions and diversification. Dorman Long expanded its bridge and construction work, securing the contract to build the prestigious Sydney Harbour Bridge. Other orders followed, including the Tyne Bridge, and Omdurman in the Sudan. Dorman Long provided the steel for prestigious buildings, including the BBC's Bush House, the new ICI headquarters, the Strand Hotel and India House. South Durham moved into the production of steel pipes.

Bolckow Vaughan, however, rarely ran at more than 50% capacity. In 1929, it merged with Dorman Long, which now became the country's largest steel manufacturer, employing 33,000 workers. The merger brought Redpath Brown under Dorman's control which, together with the acquisition in 1930 of Teesside Bridge and Engineering Works, consolidated its hold on UK steel construction. The Clarence and Newport works now closed, whilst a new coking plant was constructed at the Cleveland works. The rolling of plates was concentrated at Redcar.

By the outbreak of the Second World War in 1939 Teesside iron and steel production had regained its position. Ownership was concentrated in the hands of two major firms – only Skinningrove Ironworks retained significant independence.

More than two thirds of Dorman Long's iron, and three fifths of its steel, were now produced east of Middlesbrough. That movement speeded up after the Second World War as Dorman Long concentrated production at Redcar and Lackenby. By 1953, almost three quarters of Dorman Longs' iron and steel was made at Redcar.

Meanwhile, limited cash for investment and a growing need for a national iron and steel strategy had led in 1949 to partial nationalisation. Although this was short-lived, central control was maintained through the Iron and Steel Board.

*Top: A view inside Clarence Works foundry, c.1927. **Above** Casting pig iron at Dorman Long & Co. in 1927.*

At South Durham, a new plant for the production of steel pipes at Stockton arrived, along with major investment in the integrated works at Greatham, south of Hartlepool.

Dorman Long modernised the South Bank Cleveland Works to undertake the preparation and coking processes and opened extensive new steel making furnaces at Lackenby which led to the closure of iron and steel making at Britannia Works and Cleveland Works. The Universal Beam Mill followed in 1958. Further investment at the Cleveland Works and Lackenby continued the concentration of production in East Cleveland and led to the closure of the rolling mill at Britannia and the Acklam Works.

Dorman Long continued to be one of the world's leading bridge builders, with contracts including the Forth Road Bridge, the Tay Road Bridge and the Severn Bridge. It played a significant role in the development of atomic power stations and made many of the country's electricity pylons. Despite this, in 1967 the Labour government decided to re-nationalise the industry. The new British Steel Corporation was split into product divisions, with the remaining iron and steel works south of the river Tees, including Cleveland, Lackenby, Redcar, Britannia, Ayrton (collectively

South Teesside Works) and Cargo Fleet, along with Hartlepool and Skinningrove, becoming part of the General Steels Division.

Extensive investment at Lackenby made it one of the largest integrated steel works in the world, producing 4.5 million tonnes per annum. Older open hearth plants at Redcar, Cargo Fleet, Lackenby and Skinningrove closed; ironmaking was concentrated at Lackenby/Redcar. Improved deep water facilities at the mouth of the Tees aided the importation of large quantities of iron ore – required by the exhaustion of the Cleveland fields, the last mine closing in 1964.

In 1972, the government announced that it would invest £1,000 million in a new integrated plant at Redcar capable of producing 12 million tons per annum. Work began on the site in 1974 with the blast furnace being lit in November 1979.

Unfortunately, a world steel market recession meant the plan for a second blast furnace at Redcar was shelved and considerable job losses followed.

Throughout the 1970s, British Steel shed 21,000 jobs in the North East, leaving a workforce of just 7,000. World demand picked up in the mid-1980s and British Steel moved back into profit, leading to privatisation in 1988.

The Corporation and its Teesside works now became part of British Steel Limited, which in 1999, merged with the Dutch company Koninklijke Hoogovens to form Corus.

*Left: The Construction department at Dorman Long & Co.. The boy has just passed a white hot rivet to the engineer. **Above:** Plate shearing machine, Dorman Long & Co., Redcar, c.1930. **Below:** Cochrane's Wharf, c.1936.*

In 2003, Corus decided that the steel made at the Teesside plant was surplus to requirements, and that another outlet for its steel had to be found. This was the start of a unique 'consortium' agreement that was brokered between four international steel businesses and Corus (later to become Tata Steel).

In April 2009, however, the consortium withdrew from the agreement for Tata to supply them with steel slabs, leading to a decision to mothball the plant. The blast furnace was 'blown down' on Friday, 19 February, 2010, seemingly ending the region's steel producing history.

Geoff Waterfield, Chairman of the multi-union group, now spearheaded a 'Save Our Steel' campaign. Good news came in August 2010, when SSI signed a memorandum of understanding with Tata to buy Teesside Cast Products.

SSI was first established in 1990 as Thailand's first manufacturer of hot rolled steel sheet in coils. Since then SSI has become the largest producer of hot rolled coils in South East Asia; its President and CEO, Mr Win Viriyaprapaikit, was appointed in 2004. Despite producing an annual hot rolling capacity of 4 million tonnes per year, the goal of SSI was to become a fully integrated steel producer.

That goal was fulfilled in February 2011 when SSI signed a $469m deal with Tata Steel to buy Teesside Cast Products, and renamed it Sahaviriya Steel Industries UK (SSI UK).

At a ceremony on 25 March, 2011, Win Viriyaprapaikit was handed the Redcar Blast Furnace isolation key to mark the completion of SSI's acquisition and on 1 April, 2011, Phil Dryden joined SSI UK as Chief Executive. There followed an extensive refurbishment programme, including the relining of the Redcar Blast Furnace, giving it a campaign life of 15 to 20 years.

On 23 June, 2011, HRH The Duke of York, Prince Andrew, visited SSI UK, to mark the commencement of the start-up programme.

The Redcar Wharf, used to import raw materials, was now renamed the Redcar Bulk Terminal, becoming a joint venture company 50 percent owned by Tata Steel and 50 percent owned by SSI UK.

Sadly, Geoff Waterfield who had tirelessly campaigned for the return of steelmaking on Teesside, died suddenly in August 2011 at the age of 43.

Meanwhile, preparations to the restart of iron and steelmaking continued and generated 1,000 new direct jobs.

In October 2011, the first SSI UK new recruits attended an induction programme based around the eight key values of SSI UK: Honesty, Integrity, Respect, Excellence, Improvement, Professionalism, Transparency and Fairness.

That same month the bulk carrier the 'China Act' unloaded the first shipment of iron ore in anticipation of the resumption of ironmaking on the Redcar site. This was followed by a royal visit from HRH The Prince of Wales, Prince Charles, who visited the Redcar Blast Furnace when work was ongoing to prepare it for the re-light.

Top left: Geoff Waterfield. **Left:** *Mr Win Viriyaprapaikit and Phil Dryden, 2012.* **Above:** *HRH The Duke of York, Prince Andrew, is given a tour of the site by Phil Dryden accompanied by Win Viriyaprapaikit.* **Below:** *HRH The Prince of Wales, Prince Charles, meets Wills Waterfield during his visit in October 2011.*

On 15 April, 2012, ironmaking returned to Teesside, as Geoff Waterfield's son, Wills, performed the ceremony of lighting the Redcar Blast Furnace.

SSI UK Chief Executive Phil Dryden described bringing the plant back to life as a "titanic struggle" and spoke of Geoff Waterfield whom he said would be "remembered forever". SSI president Win Viriyaprapaikit was praised for the "vision, foresight and bravery" that he and his father Mr Wit Viriyaprapaikit had shown in purchasing the Teesside operation.

The first slab of steel was produced on 18 April, 2012. The first shipment of slabs to SSI in Thailand was celebrated, with Mr Win symbolically breaking a bottle of bubbly against some of the slabs as the loading of the vessel commenced before sailing on 15 May.

The Redcar Blast Furnace is the second biggest in Europe and is capable of producing 10,000 tonnes of iron per day, which is then converted into steel in the form of slabs.

At SSI in Thailand, the slabs are reheated and rolled into thinner hot rolled coils of steel which are used in many applications such as automotive parts and consumer products like washing machines.

Throughout its history the steel industry has played a pivotal role on Teesside. SSI UK directly employs 1,800 people, but the site's restart has also generated thousands of other jobs. The steelworks also provide significant support in the community, particularly within local schools, generating an interest that should help steelmaking thrive in the region for many more generations.

SSI UK is passionate about steel, building on Teesside's 170 years of heritage, whilst at the same time meeting the new challenges of the 21st century and consolidating the area's reputation for world class steelmaking.

Top left: Wills Waterfield relights the Blast Furnace. Left: SSI UK's first slab of steel in production. Below: Celebrating the arrival of the first slab shipment in Thailand, June 2012.

A.V. Dawson
By Road, Rail, Land and Sea

The year 2013 marked the 75th anniversary of A.V. Dawson Ltd, a Middlesbrough business with a world-wide reputation for offering import/export facilities by road, rail, land and sea. Serving customers on every continent and handling cargoes as diverse as mineral water to steel beams, the company has the expertise and experience to satisfy the most demanding clients.

Operating from sites at Dawson's Wharf, Ayrton Railhead and Store and North Sea Supply Base in Middlesbrough, the company is the largest independent dry cargo wharf operator on the River Tees.

Arthur Vernon 'Vernie' Dawson, started the firm in 1938 with the help of his wife-to-be Eleanor when they were both just 18 years old; they married a year later.

Vernie started out with just £50, raised by selling his much prized second-hand car. With the money he bought a horse named Dina, a cart for her to pull and a load of coal to sell - and he still had change. Selling coal was a full-time occupation in the winter, but during the summer Dina pulled light loads of haulage, furniture, timber and road construction materials. Despite the war business soon grew; Vernie bought a lorry and Dina went into retirement. With his new transport, it was possible to haul coal direct from the coalfields of Durham and Northumberland.

Top: Vernie's brother Jim Dawson pictured with Dina.
Left: A newly delivered 9.6 litre AEC Majestic 6 wheel lorry. All the sign writing was in gold leaf and the Dawson Shield is still in use today.

122

The Dawsons acquired six acres of land to which they would soon add five more. Shortly afterwards Vernie was taken ill and stepped down as managing director to become chairman. He never played an active role again at Middlesbrough but went on to build up a substantial farming business at Swainby, later owned and operated by his eldest grandson, Steven Dawson.

Eleanor too soon handed over her business activities and Maurice became the Managing Director.

Coal was, however, rationed and it was difficult to secure enough to meet the demand. The price of a hundredweight of coal back then was just 1/3d (6p).

Eleanor, as well as attending to everything at home, did the book-keeping and also sometimes drove the company lorries. This was necessary as many of the menfolk were away serving in the Forces.

The coal business was later sold to concentrate on road haulage, buying ex-army vehicles at first and new ones later. In 1956 Maurice Dawson, Vernie and Eleanor's son, joined them. Yet being in the haulage business wasn't easy. Vernie and Eleanor would never forget their silver wedding anniversary. It was in court in London. The Licensing Authority had refused to grant permission for additional tonnage and the couple challenged the decision. They won and celebrated the judgement and their wedding anniversary with a night out in London.

The business had been run from Emerson Street, but now it was necessary to move to larger premises at Newport Road - later home to Charlie Brown car parts. Soon that site too would be outgrown and the firm moved to Lloyd Street. But with 45 vehicles on the road that site also became too small. In 1973 the firm moved to Middlesbrough Wharf, later renamed Dawson's Wharf.

The wharf dates back to 1820 when it was called Port Darlington and served the growing steel and ironworks.

By 1980 the haulage fleet was increased by the acquisition of another Teesside haulage business, W G Thomas Ltd, raising the number of vehicles to 60.

A Heavy Haulage division had been part of the fleet since 1972, when Dawson's introduced its biggest tractor unit yet, a Scania capable of pulling 150 tonnes.

Top: *Posing for a family photograph in a borrowed MG sports car, Vernie, Eleanor, Maurice with Brenda the Alsatian and the daughter of the car's owner. This picture was taken in Emmerson Street yard in 1947.* **Left:** *A Dawson Dodge 7.5 tonne lorry with swap body furniture van.* **Below:** *A new 150hp Atkinson 6 wheel lorry carrying a load of spun cast iron pipes on behalf of Cochranes iron foundry, circa 1952.*

store potash - upwards of 20,000 tonnes. That was of interest to ICI which was looking for a place to store big bags of fertiliser. Dawson's had developed a means of lifting these with cranes which could cope with six bags at a time. Twice as efficient as the standard industry method, ICI gave Dawson's the contract. That same year the company acquired a licence to operate the wharf which had been closed for many years. The licence was limited to loading bulk, but it was enough to get Dawson's established handling ships.

The 50th anniversary of the founding of the company in 1988 coincided with the official opening of the Ayrton Store and Rail Terminal; Government Minister Michael Portillo opened it, driving into the site on the company's locomotive, the first of three. To commemorate the occasion Vernie was presented with a model 0800 locomotive by the Managing Director of British Rail. The following year Margaret Thatcher's government abolished the National Dock Labour Scheme and with that gone Dawson's was able to greatly extend its stevedoring activities.

Vernie Dawson died in 1990, shortly after his 70th birthday. Following Vernie's death the company embarked upon building its first concrete quay which was completed in 1991.

Over the next seven years the wharf saw substantial growth handling import and exports, with tonnage rising to over 400,000 tonnes a year.

To complement the tractor a Nicholas hydraulic trailer was acquired from France - the combination cost £150,000. New roads were built on the site and 30 small industrial units erected. Alas, optimism was ill-founded. Over the following three years British steel shed 22,000 jobs and the area became a ghost town. Dawson's lost 6,000 tonnes per week of road haulage; the number of vehicles fell to just 12.

In 1985 the Ayrton Rolling Mill closed with the loss of 200 jobs. Dawson's bought the site and used it to

Top left: A Volvo heavy haulage tractor with a King rear steer low-loader, transporting storage tank sections through Ripon in the late 1960s. *Left:* A Guy tractor unit with 180hp Cummins engine delivering grouser sections on behalf of BS Skinningrove in 1966. Dawsons still work for the same mill today, now owned by TATA Steel. *Above:* Heavy haulage vehicle 145 Scania with Nichola 6-axle hydraulic trailer carrying 100 tonnes of test weight blocks, 1980.

British Steel, however, moved its exports to Teesport in 1998 resulting in a massive fall in business for Dawson's. Amazingly, as a result of winning other business, only two redundancies were required; later that year an £800,000 extension to the Ayrton Railhead would be opened by the junior minister for transport Gavin Strang.

Also in 1998 the company took the huge step of purchasing the adjacent offshore fabrication yard known as Linthorpe Dinsdale, now renamed North Sea Supply Base. This enabled Dawson's to discharge larger ships of up to 7,000 tonnes and extend the quay frontage to 900 metres. The huge white fabrication halls on the site are visible throughout Teesside.

Early in 2000, the company bought new tractor units and a number of new trailers and the firm's transport fleet was back in business proudly displaying the company emblem that Vernie had developed 50 years previously - the Dawson Shield. Sadly, Eleanor was not there to see the new fleet having died in February 1999 shortly after her 80th birthday.

During 2000, it became obvious that the firm needed to improve its storage and handling facilities especially at the Ayrton International Rail Head site. The automotive contract won earlier in the year, for which Dawson's stored steel coils on behalf on British Steel, required the company to introduce heating into the huge storage buildings to stop the coils from sweating caused by changing temperatures. The firm also rented 100,000 sq ft of buildings to Cleveland Potash. Bulk potash stored loose requires good bulk walling. As a result, new walling was needed and the steel structure of the building needed protection from the potash which eats in to steel.

Extra road traffic required Dawson's to build a new road around the Ayrton site at a cost of some £3m. In addition, Freight

Facility Grants were being offered to take freight off road and onto rail. Dawson's was awarded half the £3.2m cost at the railhead site. Another expensive scheme was hard surfacing and building a new road system into the wharf sites, Dawson Wharf and North Sea Supply Base (NSSB).

Staff training, restructuring and management development now became an important issue. A senior management team consisting of 6 long-standing managers was established to drive the business forward, under the directorship of Maurice and Gary Dawson. 13 years later that same team is still in place and is headed by Andrew Watkins, Neil McShane and Russell Spink

Also in 2000, Rob Hugill became Dawson's first in-house training officer. Rob was subsequently set up in a new business, Dinsdale Risk Management Ltd, which now acts as a Health and Safety consultancy to A.V. Dawson and many of the site's tenants and other companies in the North.

In 2002, Dawson's bought the first of three Gottwald harbour cranes. The HMK 170 giving a 40 tonne lift at 25m radius was bought second hand in Venice. Gary and Maurice flew out to meet the Gottwald sales team in Venice, and after agreeing to buy the crane celebrated by drinking a glass or two of Preseco in St Mark's Square before flying home.

Meanwhile, the new business of storing automotive steel coil resulted in a new fleet of vehicles and trailers. Gary Dawson, now Managing Director, introduced a new company livery for them.

Top left: *Storage of huge steel coils on behalf on British Steel.*
Below: *Loading of deployment tower at A.V. Dawson's North Sea Supply Base.*

Diversification continued in 2004 when the firm re-invented its commercial painting business, calling it Tees Valley Coatings (TVC) for offshore and module painting, much of which was being built within the large fabrication halls at the NSSB site. TVC offers on-site tenants the opportunity to have large structures blasted, painted and metal sprayed before being shipped offshore.

Whilst in the process of renewing the haulage trailer fleet in 2004 the firm found a market for selling its old road trailers to Lagos, Nigeria. The purchase of new transport equipment and sale of the old fell to Maurice Dawson. Maurice conceived the idea of setting up a trailer hire and sales business which became Tees Valley Trailers Ltd. David Ormston joined the company and now heads a team of four people running a hire fleet of over 200 trailers whilst still selling new and used equipment in the UK and abroad.

In 2004 Dawson's took over 100% of the steel output from the British Steel (BS) plant at Skinningrove, soon to become Corus and later still TATA Steel. This plant produced some 200,000 tonnes of product, most of which was delivered by road haulage.

Another opportunity to diversify came in 2005 when Dawson's took on 42 people at the Skinningrove plant. The work involved servicing and controlling the many heavy steel rolls required daily for the rolling process. The company took on the hard task of cleaning scale from under the mill.

The first non-family director, John Young, joined the company as Financial Director in 2008. Recession hit in 2008 and within six months the company had lost 50% of turnover, falling from £12m per annum to £6m.

The steel mill at Skinningrove went from 21 shifts to just two shifts per week; steel coils stored at the Ayrton Railhead site fell from 20,000 tonnes to just 3,000 tonnes. The firm lost 28 employees. Working hours were reduced to 40 per week, and energy-saving measures were introduced.

Such measures helped save 36% of operating costs. Take-home pay was reduced by a third. Maurice wrote to all of the remaining 120 employees, keeping them informed of progress. Property owned and rented by the company helped sustain it. Only one tenant was lost. Five local sites had been acquired. The first site with a 35,000 sq ft building, a former pie factory, became a warehouse. The second was the Bowes Road Industrial Estate, now run as Bowes Road Business Park. An oil refinery site was bought and parts converted to let. The fourth site was an unused football field originally laid by Middlesbrough Council. The most recent site acquisition is a 6.5 acre plot, once part of the old Middlesbrough goods rail yard.

By 2010 the steel plant at Skinningrove was back on 18 shifts and the company was invited to offer a further service, that of cutting steel. Within 48 hours Dawson's had negotiated to buy a power-driven band saw capable of cutting to length products rolled by the Skinningrove Mill. Millserve Ltd owned by Dawson's is now a standalone company and has three such saws.

Left: Off-loading Growhow fertiliser, sixteen 1 tonne bags at a time. Above: Part of the A.V. Dawson fleet. Below: At work on Dawson's power-driven band saw.

Meanwhile, January 2010 saw the arrival of a second Gottwald harbour crane at a cost of 2.2m euros; this crane gave a lift capacity of 63 tonnes. In 2012 another Gottwald crane was acquired, a Gottwald 260. The 260 has a 100 tonnes capacity, but can also handle very large bulk grabs. The new cranes have lifted bulk loading or discharge rates to 1,000 tonnes per hour.

Also, in 2012, work on part of the former oil base was completed, transforming it into an intermodal site handling container tanks and boxes. Some 750m of new rail track was laid; the firm is now working on a new train service to the west coast for shipping containers to the USA, Canada and Italy. The whole 15 acre site is known as TRIP – the Tees Riverside Intermodal Park.

In December 2012, a total of 10 staff were given long service awards recognising over 20 years of commitment and support to the company. They had a combined total of 244 years service, the longest serving being Bob King who had driven HGVs for A.V. Dawson for 37 years.

Gary Dawson, grandson of Vernie and Eleanor, is now Managing Director, whilst Maurice Dawson is Chairman. Today, A.V. Dawson Ltd has 170 employees, and annual turnover has risen to £16m. In its 75th year the firm looks back on its past with justifiable pride, and towards the future with undiminished ambition.

*Left: Potash discharge from Ayrton Railhead. **Below:** Chairman, Maurice Dawson and Managing Director, Gary Dawson pictured in the conference room of the new administration building at the Ayrton Railhead in 2001. **Bottom:** A bird's eye view of the A.V. Dawson site.*

ATHA & CO
The One You Know

the new freedom to advertise. A radio campaign made Atha and Co into a household name on Teesside. The launch of Atha and Co onto the region's television screens was also made possible by a local TV production company.

As technology has continued to advance the company has continued to invest in its web facilities, not only providing a quick and easy way to get in touch 24 hours a day, but also including 'podcasts' which give users simple guides to understanding the process involved in making compensation claims.

Despite the march of new technology, continuity is evident at the Victorian premises of the firm's Middlesbrough office at 165, Albert Road, which have been at the heart of Atha and Co for three decades. The central location between the University and the Law Courts has proved to be as convenient for 21st century clients as for their predecessors, with the city centre well served both by public transport and car parking.

The law is a mystery to most of us. Yet sooner or later almost everyone is faced with a legal problem of some kind. Fortunately, help is at hand. The firm of Atha and Co solicitors is well known to anyone who watches regional television, listens to local radio or travels on the buses in and around Teesside.

Today, the firm specialises exclusively in Personal Injury Law covering all aspects of claims. Traffic accidents can vary from simple rear end shunts to complicated catastrophic injuries. Employment Liability Claims cover primarily accidents suffered at work, but, increasingly, Industrial Disease claims, including those arising from exposure to asbestos, form part of the firm's workload. Public Liability Claims cover a wide range of injuries suffered from simple trips in the street to accidents in public places and buildings.

The early days of laying the firm's foundations were characterised not only by long hours and hard work but also by having access to all the necessary resources locally. Local radio provided an excellent base for

Above: Tony Atha, founder of the firm. *Below:* The reception area at Atha & Co. *Facing page:* Atha & Co's 165 Albert Road, Middlesbrough, premises.

The addition of the MIMA building only adds to the prestige of the city to which Atha and Co is committed.

The story of Atha and Co began back in the early 1960s when Charles Atha's father, Tony, set up a Redcar branch of the York-based solicitors Sykes, Johnson and Lee, for whom he had originally worked as an articled clerk. Over a period of three years from a small first floor office suite in Redcar, and with the assistance of one secretary, Tony Atha conveyed over 300 properties on the Ings Farm Estate. During that period also acquired a good number of private clients. When the estate was completed, that early partnership was dissolved, leaving Tony as sole principal in the practice, which was now renamed Atha and Co.

Qualifying in 1958, after serving a two year stint of National Service as an officer in the Army, Tony Atha was admitted as a solicitor of the Supreme Court of Judicature in 1960. With construction booming across Teesside throughout the 1960s and 1970s the demand for conveyancing for both domestic and commercial properties was consistently high. The later trend of buy-to-let, and later still the introduction of the Government's Home Information Packs, would add to a steady flow of work, keeping Tony Atha and his team busy serving both homeowners and investors.

Meanwhile, Teesside's chemical and manufacturing industries were also to feature in the development of Atha and Co, when Tony's son Charles joined the practice in 1987 and began to take the firm in a new direction.

The firm successfully marketed a 'no win no fee' scheme and was years ahead of others in Teesside.

With Charles Atha at the helm the practice expanded rapidly. The growing Middlesbrough office would eventually employ five qualified solicitors, four experienced fee earners and a supporting staff of 30.

Atha & Co became one of the first firms of solicitors in England to become a corporate body recognised by the Law Society.

The 1990s saw tremendous changes to local industry as service sector jobs increased to replace the declining number of those in the manufacturing sector: the firm continued to offer Personal Injury services to those seeking to claim compensation from any quarter.

After Charles had taken his degree in Law he had decided to serve his articles with the Newcastle firm of Ward Hadway. Whilst at that time Tony Atha was disappointed that his son chose to serve his articles with another firm, that choice would prove to be exactly the right decision, since it gave Charles an insight into fields of legal work not practised by his father's firm.

The legacy of industrial diseases after decades of heavy manufacturing on Teesside left many victims suffering often painful and life-threatening conditions. They were entitled to compensation to help with costs of healthcare, and to provide for their families. That local need was the impetus for a new focus within Atha and Co as the firm geared up to win compensation for thousands of accident and industrial disease victims amid an ever increasing awareness of health and safety issues.

The industrial disease and personal injury side of the practice built up steadily. Over a decade the firm settled over 15,000 industrial deafness and other related injuries for the people of Teesside, recovering some £30 million in compensation. Eventually, however, the industrial disease work began to decline and the firm began to concentrate solely on personal injury claims.

Atha & Co are proud to say that over 70% of new clients come to them by recommendation from existing clients or through professional colleagues

Having established a knowledge base in Personal Injury, Atha and Co has developed a team of specialists focusing exclusively in that area of law. Tony Atha has now retired and today working alongside Charles Atha are company directors Rachel Maughan, Martin Demoily and Anna Guest, and solicitor Jonathan Bishop. All the directors take an active role in the management of the business as well as having their own caseload.

Regular team discussions allow the sharing of experience and joint problem solving, especially in new or particularly complex areas of law in a field which changes all the time. This level of personal involvement helps keep to a minimum the bureaucracy and red tape so often

affected them. It is only by doing this that the firm is able to negotiate the best possible compensation, ensuring that all their various losses and needs are met.

Meanwhile, the future holds a number of challenges. The Government seem determined to change the way Personal Injury claims are dealt with, with a principal aim of reducing the cost involved. This means transferring the cost from the insurer who is at fault, to the victim. The rules will change to the effect that the client is now expected to have a financial stake in the litigation and claims process and will inevitably have to make some contribution towards the cost of such from the damages received. Atha & Co will, however, continue to offer a bespoke 'No Win no Fee' service.

associated with the legal profession, and encourages a flexible and informal approach within the business.

Many clients are pleasantly surprised to have access to their own solicitor so easily, when modern business life has moved so far towards call centres and automated answering systems with several stages to get through before being able to speak to a real person.

When it comes to Personal Injury claims you can be confident Atha & Co will provide straightforward, honest but independent advice in terms that you will understand and feel comfortable to accept.

Atha and Co remains committed to being accessible and available to all those people who need help. And, whatever trends may come and go, the firm's future will remain in Teesside.

Pictures, both pages:
The Atha & Co team: Martin Demoily (top left), Anna Guest (bottom left), Rachel Maughan (above) and Charles Atha (below).

At Atha and Co direct personal contact is as much at the heart of business philosophy now as it has been since the firm began in the 1960s.

Clients seem to agree as the overwhelming majority come through personal recommendation.

Today, many Personal Injury firms have turned into little more than legal 'Factories' where claims are simply 'processed'. This most often occurs with Road Traffic Accidents where many people have their details effectively sold by their insurance companies to the companies' own panel solicitors, where their claims are dealt with by unqualified Para-Legals. Such panel solicitors are often miles from home, leaving the unfortunate client with no means of discussing matters in person with his/her solicitor, and very often finding it difficult to speak to the same person twice.

Atha & Co prides itself in getting to know clients, and getting to understand how their various injuries have

The Cleveland Centre
The Heart of Shopping

Today the Cleveland Centre is Middlesbrough's largest shopping centre. Located in the heart of Middlesbrough, it includes stores such as HMV, Boots, and Bhs as well as New Look, Top Shop and H&M.

It was back in November 1961 that property developers Norbert Sharland and Leslie Furness visited Middlesbrough to assess the possibilities of redevelopment on a major scale. Neither knew the area well, so they spent many hours walking the town, watching the pedestrian flow, debating the merits of one site rather than another.

The two men decided on the area bounded by Linthorpe Road, Bottomley Street, Fletcher Street and Fallows Street which seemed a 'natural' area for shopping renewal and extension, absorbing the less valuable parts to the rear of Linthorpe Road to compensate for some of the very expensive property that would need to be bought on Linthorpe Road. As a result the established pedestrian flow through Newton Street would be maintained on redevelopment.

Messrs Sharland and Furness carefully investigated the commercial and social requirements of the project and made detailed financial plans to fund the work. They appointed architects Turner, Lansdowne, Holt and Partners, then set about negotiations with the owners of the properties they would need to acquire.

Within a few months the pair had negotiated contracts to buy several important properties. Now they needed to 'sell' their idea for development to a finance company willing to lend the estimated £3 million needed to make it happen. In due course an investment company, Barratt-Victoria (Middlesbrough) Property Company Ltd was formed.

The Borough Engineer and Surveyor approved plans submitted in April 1962, but they wanted the scheme enlarged to include Albert Road. As a result the scheme was enlarged to co-ordinate with plans to rebuild between Wesley Street and Fallows Street.

By March 1963 the Arndale Property Trust had submitted plans for a mammoth £10 million scheme stretching from Borough Road to Corporation Road. Perhaps feeling that the idea had grown too big, Barratt-Victoria submitted a third scheme. After several meetings, it was decided that Barratt-Victoria and Arndale would each proceed independently to develop the sites each owned. Co-operation seemed sensible since the substantial ownership of property already established would involve the minimum use of compulsory purchase powers. However, it was not to be. The council decided it wished to deal with a single company or consortium as developer, and wanted unified ownership of the whole area. Arndale now decided not to pursue the scheme it had submitted the previous year. It was not until the summer of 1965, after Turner, Lansdowne, Holt & Partners had produced several variations on their plans, that the Council felt able to agree in principle to the scheme. The redevelopment area by now extended to six acres.

Barratt-Victoria had a strong team. Its architects were sensitive to what would blend in well with the surrounding area of town. The company was sensible enough to produce ideas that could be afforded, and experienced enough to cope with all the construction problems.

Facing page, top: Construction of the Cleveland Centre begins in 1970. *Facing page bottom, and above:* Exterior views of the Cleveland Centre in the 1980s and 1990s. *Below:* The Centre's model replica of Captain Cook's ship, *Endeavour.*

Building started in July 1969. Six streets made way for the Cleveland Centre, but those streets were not forgotten. The top half of Fletcher Street became the entrance to the centre for service vehicles to the first floor, and for shoppers' cars going to the second floor parking area. Two of the climate-controlled shopping malls would be named after Newton and Wesley Streets.

Development took ten years from conception to completion, at a cost of £4m. Construction was in three phases, the first opening in 1970 and covering some Linthorpe Road perimeter shops. In 1972 the second phase began with the opening of Newton Mall for the benefit of one shop: others, however, quickly followed. On completion of the third phase in 1973 there were 318,000 square feet of retail in a total 494,180 square feet.

The Council intended to become the ground landlord, but private enterprise would acquire by agreement a multitude of other property interests. Public roads ran through the site which would have to be closed, and so it now became necessary to compulsorily acquire the land. The compulsory purchasing involved exacting and time-consuming procedures under the Town and Country Planning Act. Numerous detailed plans were prepared, together with documents and reports. It was almost Christmas 1966 before the local authority formally submitted its proposals to the Minister of Housing and Local Government.

The necessary public enquiry was held in September 1967. A public exhibition had been held previously; affected traders had been promised rehousing in the new scheme with continuity of trading wherever possible. There were therefore few objections, and the Minister's approval to go ahead with the project was given in 1968.

Promises to traders were kept. For example, the old Erimus public house was not demolished before new licensed premises were put up for Vaux Breweries, and the National Westminster Bank was temporarily rehoused.

By the early 1980s it was clear that the Centre had become outdated through normal wear and tear, and through changes in legislation concerning fire and health and safety. It was now that the Legal and General Assurance Company acquired the Centre. Legal and General appointed Bradshaw, Rowse and Harker as architects for a refurbishment programme carried out during 1984-6. It added 7,000 square feet of new retail space at a cost of more than £7 million. The Centre now consisted of 86 units incorporating a wine bar, restaurants, a roof top nightclub, three office blocks, a very large Health Centre and a car park with 550 spaces, leased to the local authority.

In 1997 Legal and General again commissioned Bradshaw, Rowse and Harker to give the Centre a cosmetic uplift costing £3.5 million. This involved laying new floors throughout giving a much lighter appearance. This was followed by new ceilings with incorporated lighting. Cladding and other new wall finishes were added, together with new signs and graphics to reflect the Centre's modern image.

The Centre team was strengthened by a new general manager who made it her mission to bring the Cleveland Centre back into the heart of the community. A first came in August 2012 when the Centre welcomed Mickey and Minnie Mouse all the way from Disney World, Florida; the free event for shoppers attracted thousands. That same year the Centre raised over £12,000 to support two guide dog puppies through training, Lola and Sadie would be placed with local families in 2013.

Meanwhile, plans continue for a new development of a food court, and the run-down vacant offices and shops on Albert Road which it is hoped to transform into a hotel in 2013.

Continued investment has seen the Cleveland Centre develop as a major shopping venue, ensuring that Middlesbrough remains the destination of choice for the wider Tees Valley.

Facing page, top: Development of The Mall. ***Facing page, bottom:*** *Interior views of The Mall in 2007.* **Above and below:** *Inside the new Cleveland Centre in 2012.* **Left:** *New branding of the Cleveland Centre.*

Improvements were made to most of the entrances, and the area known as Cleveland Square was completely revamped, drawing all eyes to the main focal point, a one fifth-scale model of Captain Cook's ship, Endeavour. Wall graphics depicting a seascape and harbour scene, and an attractive new feature, a map of one of Cook's voyages, was set in the floor and lit by fibre optics.

The Cleveland Shopping Centre was bought by The Mall Corporation, the country's leading owner and developer of community shopping centres, in September 2004. Shortly after the purchase, The Mall Corporation embarked on another multi-million pound development which included the reconfiguration of Cleveland Square and the development of the former Littlewoods department store. In total 80,000 square feet of retail space was developed, attracting new retailers to the town. As part of the development the owners also took the opportunity to improve the internal decorations and facilities which helped attract a host of new retailers and customers.

In October 2006, what was now called 'The Mall' bought the rights to operate the roof top car park, redeveloping it to provide modern and safe facilities for visitors. Development continued in 2009 with a £1m refurbishment to Barclays Bank in Corporation Road, a striking new glass building.

Ownership of 'The Mall' changed again in September 2011 when the centre was sold to private investors who changed the name back to the Cleveland Centre.

In January 2012, the rebrand commenced and the pink 'Mall' signs disappeared. New stores soon appeared including the 99p Store and the premium Apple technology retailer Stormfront.

Fawcett & Hetherington
A Final Service

Bereavement is always a difficult time for families. It is a time when people are often confused and distressed; a time when a helping hand from someone who knows what to do is most needed, and is most welcome.

It was out of this universal need, one common to all people in all cultures throughout history, that there arose the profession of undertaker.

The professional undertaker today, however, is far removed from those persons who might have taken on that role a century ago – or even less. For ordinary folk before the Great War it was very often a local woman, often also the local midwife, who might be given the task of laying out the departed.

A coffin might well be commissioned simply from the local joiner. As for a chapel of rest – very likely that would just be the front room, or for those who had no front room then the kitchen, perhaps the only room they had.

Undertakers did exist of course, but there were simply far fewer of them. But times moved on; many of the joiners who made coffins branched out to become fully fledged undertakers, the origin of many of today's firms. Meanwhile, other firms began to emerge from other professional routes,

such as taxi proprietors, as the need and demand for better quality funeral services became apparent as the twentieth century progressed.

Today, one of the best known local firms of family undertakers is Fawcett & Hetherington Funeral Services.

The company opened for business on the 14 June, 1993. It was founded by Alistair Fawcett and David Hetherington. David was the third generation of his family to work in the funeral profession. David and Alistair had both previously worked together at the Co-operative Funeral Service before starting up their own funeral firm.

When the company started the pair hired cars for three months, until they could purchase their first hearse and limousine. Since then there has been a succession of vehicles down the years, and now the company owns two hearses, three limousines and two general purpose vehicles.

Above and left: *The firm's old premises at 15, High Street, Normanby (above) and 120 Normanby Road, South Bank (left).* ***Below, left to right:*** *David Hetherington, Margaret Lumsden (nee Hetherington) Alistair Fawcett and Pauline Fawcett.*

Eston, Middlesbrough, where the firm is now based, had previously been a pub called 'The George'. Despite its change of use the firm kept one historical reminder of the pub - calling the new premises 'King George House'.

Meanwhile, the family story continued. In 2011 Terry's wife, Joanne, joined the company to help in the office, and in 2012 Pauline's brother-in-law, David Green, started in the firm helping with coffins and driving.

At the start there were two partners Alistair and David, who shared funeral directing, embalming, coffin making and driving whilst David's sister Margaret ran the office. There was, however, always a selection of on-call drivers also employed by the business in order to be able to provide a complete funeral service no matter how many staff might be needed to help.

Fawcett & Hetherington's first premises back in 1993 were at 120 Normanby Road, South Bank; these remained in operation until 2010. Soon after the firm started there was also another funeral home at 15, High Street, Normanby, which was opened in 1995.

From the outset the company always has been a family business. Pauline Fawcett, Alistair's wife, joined in 1994 to help out in the office as the business began to take off.

David Hetherington retired in 2004 and Alistair took full control of the business. David's sister Margaret also soon retired. Alistair's eldest son, Terry, now joined the business to train as a funeral director and to complete the coffin work. In 2008, Alistair's youngest son, Andrew, joined the business to train as an embalmer and to work in the office. Andrew's arrival meant the whole of Alistair's family was now involved in the business, and the company comprised two generations of the Fawcett family.

The two original premises eventually closed in 2010 when the company bought, redeveloped and moved into new premises in Eston. The new funeral home at 92, High Street,

That family theme also extends to the firm's attitude to its business. The company's number one priority is customer service and being a valued member of the community, 'Our Family Caring for Your Family' features on the firm's advertising material, as this is exactly what the Fawcett family feel their role should be.

Although the firm was founded in the 1990s the nature of the business provides many opportunities to reflect on the past, not least on the Second World War and the generation which is now passing.

Top left and above: A Victorian view of the former King George IV Inn (top left) which after major renovations is the new home of Fawcett & Hetherington, pictured above in 2012. **Below:** *The family today, L-R: Andrew, Pauline, Alistair, Joanne and Terry and the Fawcett & Hetherington motto - Our Family Caring for Your Family.*

Our Family, Caring For Your Family

But Heinrich Richter's body was only found when builders unearthed the plane's wreckage in December 1997. Fragments of a name tag and German war records identified the body as that of pilot Heinrich Richter.

British veterans attended the funeral and subsequent burial at Thornaby Cemetery in Teesside - along with the German Consul General Hans Mordorf and diplomatic officials.

The funeral service was said in both German and English at St Peter's Church in Middlesbrough - just 400m from where his plane crashed.

Another unusual commission came in 2003 when Fawcett & Hetherington provided a casket to house the remains of Saint Eugenia of Rome, who was beheaded on December 25, 258AD, being martyred for her faith. Her remains had been held safe in a local church and the casket was provided to repatriate those remains to her home city of Rome. The firm received special thanks from the local priest and the Bishop of Middlesbrough.

Not every client from that generation, however, is someone whom one might expect.

In 1998 Fawcett & Hetherington directed the funeral of a German pilot who was killed in action over Middlesbrough in 1942 when his plane was shot down. His remains had lain undiscovered for 52 years.

Although few final journeys involve the expense of a trip to Rome, the costs of a funeral service have increased dramatically over the two decades that the firm has been in existence. However, at Fawcett & Hetherington every effort is made to ensure those ever increasing costs are not always passed on, and the firm prides itself on not only having a very customer-focused business, but also one that provides better value for money than similar enterprises in the same area.

Heinrich Richter was on a raid to bomb the Skinningrove Ironworks on Teesside when his plane was brought down. He was aged 31.

At the time, three crewmen were found near the wreckage and subsequently buried locally.

This page: Views inside the newly renovated King George House: the Chapel of Rest (top left), the Main Area (left), the General Office (bottom left) and the Service Chapel (below).

These days even the environment is a consideration. The firm is believed to be the only Funeral Service in the Tees Valley area to offer 'The Coffin Cover', which is a low cost, sustainable and dignified alternative to a traditional coffin.

The firm can help clients choose a lasting memorial and guide them through the process step-by-step. There are a large range of memorials to choose from and all styles, carvings and type of stone can be interchanged as required. Though it can take about 12 weeks for a memorial to be erected it is worth the wait. Staff can also arrange having any additional inscriptions, cleaning, repairing, re-gilding, re-painting to existing memorials.

The firm offers a full range of Pre-Payment Funeral Options that are organised through the Perfect Choice organisation. Fawcett & Hetherington tailors each funeral plan to the client's specific needs and requirements and provides free no-obligation estimates for consideration. This service is easy to arrange and is conducted in a meeting with one of the firm's funeral directors

At the firm's premises are six chapels of rest, two of which were specifically designed to provide for disabled access. There is also a Service Chapel in which can be held small Funeral Services and other related activities. Those wishing to use the facility need only to contact the firm.

As for transport, Fawcett & Hetherington not only has its own fleet of Mercedes funeral vehicles but can also even supply a Horse Drawn Hearse should one be requested.

As for professional standards, none come higher.

Fawcett & Hetherington is a member of the National Association of Funeral Directors and strictly abides by its Code of Practice. The firm's staff are also individually members of the British Institute of Funeral Directors and the British Institute of Embalmers and abide wholly by their strict standards of professional practice.

Throughout Fawcett & Hetherington always aims to ensure that their final service is the best service.

Top left: Fawcett and Hetherington's horse-drawn hearse. *Centre:* A selection of the firm's memorials. *Below:* Part of the Fawcett & Hetherington Mercedes fleet.

Fawcett & Hetherington Funeral Service would like to thank Paul Terry for kindly taking and supplying a number of the photographs in this article.

R C Ayres
Building a Reputation

The building trade is probably the world's second oldest profession. According to the Masons the profession doesn't just go back to the builders of Solomon's temple but traces its origins all the way back to those skilled tradesmen who worked on building the great pyramids of Egypt.

Of course, you won't find many pyramids on Teesside, but there are countless buildings, both old and modern, which are a testament to the skills and expertise of local craftsmen.

If was the Romans who first brought tradesmen skilled in building in stone, brick and tile to northern England – then known as the Roman province of Britannia.

It wasn't, however, until the Victorian era that a building boom began on the banks of the Tees that has, despite wars and intermittent recessions, continued to this day.

Today, R C Ayres Building and Roofing Services Ltd, based at Cranston House, Douglas Street, Middlesbrough, continues that tradition, mixing traditional skills and experience with the very best of the new.

In 1915, having completed his apprenticeship as a slater and tiler, Charles Henry Ayres bought himself a handcart for three shillings and nine pence and so began the family business that still exists today.

Charles set up his slating and tiling firm in a small part of a large commercial site in Douglas Street, walking to his first jobs, pushing the handcart loaded with roofing materials. Luckily, he was a strong man, keen on bodybuilding and winner of third prize in a 'Mr. Yorkshire' bodybuilding contest.

The First World War had taken many men away from the building industry. As a result, in 1918, at the war's end there was a long backlog of work to be done. With men returning to life in Civvy Street, long delayed marriages were happening all around, and with them came a demand for extra homes for new families.

*Above: Founder Charles Henry Ayres. **Below:** Charles Ayres (in white sleeves) and a colleague on a roofing job in Bishop Auckland in 1910.*

Scottish and Newcastle Breweries were two of the important clients who used R.C. Ayres' services for many years. Elsewhere, as part of their work refurbishing the Coatham Hotel in Redcar in 1962, the company removed the gun turrets erected during the First World War from the hotel tower.

Attracting a growing and loyal workforce, the company acquired a reputation for specialist roofing skills and excellent workmanship. Ted Dunn and Joe McMahon underwent their apprenticeship as slaters and tilers at R C Ayres and went on to spend their whole working lives with the company, notching up over 90 years between them. In 1962, they took Ronald's son, Alan Charles, under their wing when he became the third generation to work in the family firm.

Alan Ayres, the current owner and managing director of the company, remembers how different life in the building and roofing industry was when he started work for the company: "There was a lime pit in the yard where lime was slaked ready for use, and bricks arrived still hot from Coatham Stob Brickworks and all had to be unloaded and stacked by hand".

Though it would later be overshadowed by the long economic depression of the 'Hungry Thirties', the 'Roaring Twenties' was a decade of economic boom.

And by the 1920s Charlie Ayres was employing eight men. His eldest son, Ronald Cranston Ayres, followed in his father's footsteps, joining the business as an apprentice slater and tiler in the less busy decade of the 1930s.

Ron left the company to join the armed forces, along with his two younger brothers, Stanley Charles and Edgar, when the Second World War broke out in 1939. Charlie, meanwhile, continued to work in the business until 1940 when, sadly, while his sons were away, he suffered a heart attack and died.

As a result of Charlie's death the company ceased trading, but in 1946 Ron, who survived Dunkirk, was demobbed from the army. He decided to re-start the business under his own name, R C Ayres. He was joined for a short time by his brothers - Stan as a bricklayer, and Edgar as a wagon driver. Ron's wife, Nora, managed the office.

In the post-war years Ron built a thriving business which saw a welcome development in the transportation of men and materials: a motor vehicle. In the days of the handcart, when jobs were carried out in Thornaby, a fortifying tea-break was taken before tackling the challenge of Brewery Bank!

The company carried out major building and roofing works for a variety of clients including heavy industry, commercial enterprises and local authority, domestic and heritage projects. Head Wrightson's Steel Foundry and

*Top left: Re-roofing and refurbishment of the County Hotel in Newport Road in the late 1950s. **Above**: Refurbishment of the Old Town Hall, Middlesbrough which gained the company a Civic Award in 1984. **Below**: Second generation Ron Ayres, far right and third generation Alan Ayres, second from right, present workers Joe McMahon and Ted Dunn with 25 years service watches, 1978.*

Mechanical and motorised assistance with lifting and moving heavy gear wasn't as readily available as it is now. Work was hard but there was camaraderie among the men and lots of good humour.

Alan took over the running of the business in 1972 when his father Ron became ill. The company continued to grow and gradually acquired the whole Douglas Street site, land and buildings, including Brine Wells Garage which was accessible from Borough Road. Joinery goods were manufactured on site and motor mechanics employed to maintain vehicles, plant and equipment.

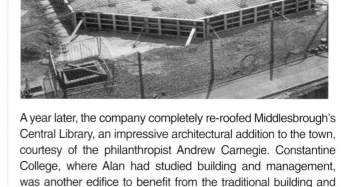

The skills of Ted, Joe, George Barrass (bricklayer), Bob Eden and Bill Earl (joiners), Tommy Wardle (general foreman) and many other long-serving employees, meant that the company won a number of prestigious orders. In 1984 the firm was presented with a Civic Award for the restoration of the original Middlesbrough Town Hall.

A year later, the company completely re-roofed Middlesbrough's Central Library, an impressive architectural addition to the town, courtesy of the philanthropist Andrew Carnegie. Constantine College, where Alan had studied building and management, was another edifice to benefit from the traditional building and roofing skills which were the trademark of the company.

Top and above: A recent project for Growhow UK Ltd, the installation of a fixed fire protection system including concrete bases for water tanks bases supported by 104 18m deep piles at their Billingham Plant. *Left:* Koppers pitch shed. R C Ayres over sprayed the 3000m2 pitch storage shed roof with a liquid rubber waterproof coating.

lawyer specialising in construction and Rachael who has a doctorate in Clinical Psychology works for a management consultancy company. Sue, sister of Alan's wife, Elizabeth, is part of the administrative support team in the company offices.

The dual focus - building and roofing - of the firm continues to this day operating on the Wilton & Billingham Chemical complexes and clients throughout the area.

Clients include: Amec, Davy Process Technology, Fabrick Housing Group, Growhow UK Ltd, Johnson Matthey Ltd, Koppers UK Ltd, Lotte Chemicals Ltd, Sabic UK Ltd, Sembcorp Uk Ltd and Teesside University.

Later the business was highly commended in the National Heritage Awards for the 1995 restoration of Ivy Cottage, a long house in Cowpen Bewley and the oldest dwelling house in Cleveland. This was a Cleveland Preservation Society project. The Analytical Chemists, Ridsdale and Co., also needed a company that had retained traditional slating skills when Newham Hall at Newby required work on the old Westmoreland slated roof.

R C Ayres Building and Roofing Services Ltd enjoys an enviable reputation for construction and civil engineering in the commercial sector. Founded in 1915, for a century now the firm has been providing a high quality of service to its clients. Today, that well earned reputation is higher than ever.

Alongside traditional skills R C Ayres kept up with modern developments and was at the forefront of the flat roofing revolution. More durable single ply P.V.C. membranes are now replacing the traditional felt roofing products. Alan and a number of employees went to Switzerland in 1983 for training in the use of such advanced products and have since used them regularly to cure leaky flat roofs on schools, hospitals and vast areas such as the 15,000 square metre roof of Next Distribution warehouses near Tilbury Docks.

Above: Recent R C Ayres project - partial re-roofing of Sembcorp Utilities UK's Wilton Power Station. *Below: The newly-weds - a happy day for the Ayres family in September 2012. Left to right: Michael Ayres, Elizabeth Ayres, Sean Parry (groom), Rachael Ayres (now Parry) and Alan Ayres.*

Alan felt that his involvement with the Erimus Decent Homes Project brought the company, in some respects, full circle, as some of the houses his father Ron Ayres tiled in Linthorpe were repaired and re-roofed by the company some seventy years later. The roofs had, like the company, stood the test of time.

Family continues to be a recurring theme in the business. Alan's son, Michael, and daughter Rachael, worked at Douglas Street during their student days - thus four generations have now worked for the company - though today Michael is a

QA Weld Tech
Quality Assured Welding Technology

QA Weld Tech Limited is based on Bowes Road, on Middlesbrough's Riverside Park Industrial Estate. The Company operates primarily within the Offshore Oil & Gas Sector supplying integrated engineering solutions and turnkey manufacture of critical and technically demanding equipment to an international clientele.

With its staff of fully qualified welding engineers, metallurgists, coded welders, experienced fabricators and CNC machinists, the company can apply an extensive range of processes and procedures on materials ranging from carbon and low alloy steel, through to the duplex stainless steels and high nickel alloys.

QA Weld Tech Ltd (QAWT) was founded in 1980 on the same day as a national steel strike was announced – an inauspicious start for an engineering business hoping to have the British Steel Corporation as a key customer.

The company started business on the then newly developed Riverside Park Industrial Estate, which was the original 'Iron Masters' district and the birth place of industrial Middlesbrough. The two founders, Charles Tighe and Mervyn Jones, had each been employed at local heavy engineering companies, Head Wrightson, 'Heads', and Whessoe, with long careers as welding engineers, after serving their time together in Head Wrightson's Research and Development division. As Charles says, "Heads was a wonderful training ground, and whilst we didn't realise it at the time, it truly was an investor in people".

Charles and Mervyn lost contact for a few years, Charles becoming Chief Welding Engineer at 'Heads' and Mervyn going on to BSC, where, in his words, "they tried to set fire to me with a ladle of molten steel" prompting him to leave BSC and pursue a career as a Welding Metallurgist at Whessoe and then finally as a technical sales representative with a welding consumable company. It was at this point they met up again and formed the idea of setting up in business together.

The pair recognised the opportunity for a small specialist company offering a technical welding service and set up QAWT.

Top: Charles Tighe, joint founder of Q A Weld Tech Ltd. *Left:* QAWT was the first business to open on Riverside Park Industrial Estate in February 1980. *Above:* The first job for QAWT was for Northern Valve Services at ICI Wilton.

QAWT's market is primarily coded and technically demanding welding for the Offshore, Petrochemical and General Engineering industries, but by far its largest business sector is the manufacture of high pressure pipe flowspools and associated equipment for sub-sea wellhead 'Christmas Trees' and manifolds (In the drilling industry a 'Christmas Tree' is an assembly of valves, spools, and fittings used for an oil well. It is named for its rough resemblance to a decorated tree. Its function is to control the flow out of the well).

The company was the first business to start trading on Riverside Park in Unit 1A, a 6,000 sq ft factory unit on Bowes Road. As well as the two directors, they employed one office girl, two welders and a plater. In their haste to get the business underway, they moved into 1A without electricity, which was 'a bit tricky' for a welding company, and had to rent diesel generators until electrical supplies were connected.

The oil and gas sub-sea market has provided the company with its main customers and business opportunity for the past 30 years, and has allowed the business to progress from a specialist welding company providing a sub-contract welding service to Teesside engineering companies, to today being an integrated engineering business supplying turnkey solutions to a global clientele.

The firm's first order was for a valve piping module for ICI, and their customer, a local valve stockists, not only delivered the pipe and valves for welding-up but was persuaded to collect the assembly benches to enable the work to be carried out. The office was Mervyn's caravan strategically positioned inside the workshop.

Mervyn Jones retired from QAWT in 2003, but led by Charles Tighe the company continued to prosper, and over the ensuing years it has grown progressively and now occupies all eight of the factory units in the original courtyard and has over 60 employees. Further expansion and growth is expected over the next few years with investment in people, processes and capacity to meet world-wide sales.

There has always been an active apprentice scheme within the company and its first apprentice welder, Peter Harrison, who started in 1983, has progressed to Welding Engineer and received his 25 year

More than 50% of the sales are for export to Europe, from Sweden to Romania, the USA, Australia, Singapore and Malaysia, Africa, from Egypt to Democratic Republic of Congo, and more recently to the booming economy of Brazil.

Top left: "Inches to spare", Mervyn Jones guides a bull wheel for BSC Redcar into the workshop. **Above:** Gordon Saul at work. Gordon started at QAWT in 1982 as a driver labourer and over his career progressed to Inspection Technician and was the first employee to receive a 25 year long service award in 2007. **Left:** Stan Naisbitt inspecting the Rotating Chute for Redcar Blast Furnace.

With a build cost of £2.3 million Big Geordie, also known as 'BE 1550W', the famous excavator was once Western Europe's biggest muck shifter.

The excavator had arrived in Northumberland in 1969 where its huge shovel rapidly gouged away surface earth to expose seams of coal below. Visitors from all over the world came to see Big Geordie in its prime.

This planned capacity manufacture wasn't always the case, and in the early days, many challenges were undertaken to establish the business. No job was considered too big, as long as it had a 'technical welding' content. Steel castings were sent over to the Riverside Park factory and the welding was carried out on the back of the wagon if it couldn't be offloaded into the workshop - or welders would be sent out to carry out the assembly and welding in the customer's own works.

If large heavy items had to be welded inside, cranes would be rented to offload and position the item inside the workshop, often with only inches to spare to get the part inside the door.

On-site welding was often undertaken and QAWT worked on many of the major sites around Teesside including BSC, Tioxide, Shell Teesport, ICI and Enron, many of which are no longer around. A regular repair and maintenance contract in those early days was repairing the biggest walking dragline in Western Europe, 'Big Geordie', which was then working the Butterwell Open Cast coal site in Northumberland.

Big Geordie worked on some of the UK's biggest opencast mining sites including Widdrington, Butterwell and finally Stobswood.

Big Geordie was powered by electricity and weighed 3,000 tonnes. With its jib fully extended straight up it reached a height of almost 260 feet. The dragline excavator had a bucket big enough for three cars to park inside or gouge out 100 tons of earth with a single bite. Backed up against one of the goals at Wembley Stadium, Big Geordie could have thrown its excavator bucket into the penalty box at the other end of the pitch. It certainly couldn't have run down the pitch to score a goal, however!

The monster excavator moved at a speed of just two metres a minute on giant pontoon feet that lifted its body off the ground before lowering it a few feet ahead.

*Top, left and right: 1982, working on the biggest walking dragline in Western Europe, 'Big Geordie' at Butterwell Open Cast coal site in Northumberland. **Left:** Many changes have taken place in the 30 plus years the company has been going, including improving the working environment to modern industrial workshops. **Left inset:** A new venture into CNC Machining in 2007.*

Impressing the judges in areas of quality, innovation, investment in people and equipment, sales performance, and markets served, the award recognised the achievements of the 60-strong workforce over the preceding 12 months.

Charles Tighe said "The whole Company is tremendously proud to have won this award. We have gone through a period of unprecedented growth in the last three years, investing in both personnel and equipment to make sure that we are ready to meet the challenges the engineering industry faces in the forthcoming years. We are delighted that these efforts have been recognised."

The huge industrial excavator dominated the Northumberland skyline for years, but sadly, with no interest from other mining companies, the decision was made in 2004 to dismantle it.

By then, however, QAWT had grown and diversified, finding its own particular niche within the offshore oil and gas sector. To do so it had to introduce and conform to the many and varied Quality, HSE and Environmental management systems required by both legislation and the industry. The early, exciting challenges had to be curtailed to allow the company to progress and aspire to its current market position. This in itself resulted in more business opportunities, and as the company achieved the various ISO Standards in Quality, HSE and Environment, so it received many customer awards for manufacturing excellence, quality, delivery and innovation whilst providing secure and stable employment for over 30 years.

Fighting off strong competition, QA Weld Tech won the 2012 Manufacturer of the Year title for the Teesside region at the prestigious NE Business Awards, held at Teesside University.

Top left: During 2010, the company upgraded the workshops and constructed a new office block. Left: Peter Harrison who was the company's first apprentice welder in 1983. Having progressed from apprentice to welder to Team Leader, he is now Company Welding Engineer. Peter received a 25 year long service award in 2008. Bottom left: QAWT has won a number of Client Awards for their commitment to quality, delivery and HSE. Above: Staff commemorate the opening of the new offices in March 2011. Below: Charles Tighe receives the award on behalf of the company as Manufacturer of the Year for 2012 at the Teesside Business Awards.

Geoffrey Robinson
Energy Solutions

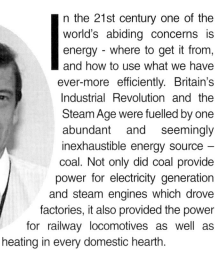

In the 21st century one of the world's abiding concerns is energy - where to get it from, and how to use what we have ever-more efficiently. Britain's Industrial Revolution and the Steam Age were fuelled by one abundant and seemingly inexhaustible energy source – coal. Not only did coal provide power for electricity generation and steam engines which drove factories, it also provided the power for railway locomotives as well as heating in every domestic hearth.

Coal also turned out to be of value when processed into another form of energy: town gas.

When heated in the absence of oxygen coal gives off flammable fumes 'town gas' which once collected in gasholders, could be piped anywhere.

Gas lighting became a common feature of Victorian England; and gaslights would remain a familiar sight in our streets until the 1960s. And, although electric lighting would eventually take over, gas still remained a favoured way of providing heating, cooking and process heating – not least as Clean Air Acts encouraged the displacement of coal as the most common form of fuel.

With almost miraculous timing natural gas and oil were discovered in the North Sea. However, the problem was that all gas fired equipment was designed to run on 'town gas', and so every single appliance, furnace and oven now needed to be converted to operate using the newly available 'North Sea' gas.

About 40 million appliances of all types were converted in the programme, throughout the UK. With the vast scale of this task, the conversion programme started with an initial trial area in May 1967 in Burton on Trent, Derbyshire. When completed the results of this trial were analyzed by the various Gas Boards, formulating best conversion practice before embarking on the national conversion program which was finally completed in 1977. It was hugely expensive for British Gas, costing £563 million.

On the day of the changeover, all customers in the area were required to switch off their appliances and the old town gas was purged from the local mains system. In the industrial premises, gas engineers were allocated the responsibility for supervising a given factory conversion.

Top left: Founder, Geoffrey Robinson. Top right: The first purpose-built offices/workshop on the Cowpen Estate. Above: George Cheetham, one of Geoffrey Robinson's earliest craftsmen. Left: Jointing a gas pipe alongside an early company vehicle.

Geoffrey Robinson, founder of Geoffrey Robinson Ltd now based in Macklin Avenue, on the Cowpen Industrial Estate at Billingham, began his career as an apprentice fuel technologist in the Fuel & Furnace Research Department, at Swindon Laboratories, back in 1962. With the advent of natural gas, Geoffrey joined the East Midlands Gas Board industrial conversion team and worked on that first pilot conversion project at Burton on Trent. He then joined Seaflame to work on industrial and commercial conversion projects in the greater London area. With Seaflame Geoffrey later moved to Darlington to undertake second phase conversion works, converting coal and heavy fuel oil plant to natural gas and dual fuel.

In 1971, when Seaflame pulled back to London Geoffrey formed Geoffrey Robinson Ltd., initially to continue the gas conversion work.

The new company started with an office in Hutton Rudby before moving to a converted shop on The Green, at Billingham.

In the early years, there was a very close working relationship with the Gas Regions, with whom Geoffrey Robinson Ltd or 'GRL' operated as a specialist contractor benefiting from his experience in the new technological developments gained in the conversion experience.

For Workington Iron & Steel Co. the company undertook the changeover of all the gas equipment in the works from town to natural gas. This included its industrial process burners as well as the commercial equipment. Later for this company, GRL designed, manufactured and installed a furnace to heat treat 12 tons of steel rolls. Here GRL was the only company able to meet the tight delivery deadline set by the client.

On larger sites it was normal practice to locate the gas meter on the site boundary and then run underground to the boiler house.

This coincided with the introduction of polyethylene gas piping. This was originally supplied in imperial sizes as GRL used to deliver gas throughout Gosforth Park. Later the piping changed to metric sizes. GRL was so involved in the early use of this new material that it had one of the first 250 mm 'butt fusion' machines even before they were delivered to the local Gas Board.

Conversion experience led into the changeover of existing boiler plant to natural gas firing and dual fuel firing. This in turn led into the installation of underground PE Gas and water mains. This developed into an expertise in large boiler plant and steam installations.

Top left: Workers cutting up a Lancashire Boiler at South Shields General. Top right: One of the last pulversided coal fired boilers in any hospital being removed from Newcastle General. Left: Laying the gas main for the James Cook Hospital. Above: Fabricated chimney sections ready for delivery to site.

As the company grew it became clear that it needed to offer a broader range of Building Engineering Services; as a result, engineers joined the firm to bring in additional skills. As GRL grew it relocated to purpose-built premises on the Cowpen Industrial Estate: and when it outgrew those it moved across the road to its second purpose-built, current site.

The additional services that were developed included electrical engineering, ductwork manufacture, insulation installation and plumbing.

Maintaining its involvement with the efficient use of energy, the firm currently offers clients a comprehensive range of renewable energy schemes, including Biomass Heating, Biomass CHP, Solar P V and Solar Thermal.

Similarly for Carbon Reduction GRL offers low energy lighting, high efficiency burners and energy reduction schemes. One

example is the Friarage Hospital at Northallerton. There GRL constructed and operates a new energy center which is saving 20% in energy consumption when compared with the old boiler plant.

The very first job undertaken by GRL, back in 1971, was the conversion of Whinney House Hospital from coal to gas firing. Since then the company has maintained an involvement with various Health Trusts including the mechanical services for the RVI Newcastle new main hospital block.

In recent years GRL has been the market leader in hospital energy centre installations and upgrades in the North East, having refurbished and replaced plant in 90% of the North East hospitals including:-Royal Victoria Infirmary Energy Centre - a full installation for Dalkia; Freeman Hospital Energy Centre - a steam plant upgrade for Dalkia; Sunderland Royal Hospital - a full installation for Sunderland Health Service: Friarage Hospital

Northallerton - a full installation as part of a PPP for South Tees NHS Trust; Newcastle General Hospital - a Full Installation for the Trust and for South Tyneside Health Trust projects included the boiler replacement/conversion and ward Installations at South Tyneside General Hospital.

Also, at James Cook University Hospital the company installed water services and the gas pipe work for the energy centre at the start of construction. Later they also provided pipe work Upgrades for the Trust's energy provider.

In late 2003, an electrical department was introduced to the company, with a new manager appointed in February 2004, he is still with the company on the Board of Directors.

Left: The Biomass CHP plant at Wilton. Below left: Improving energy efficiency at Friarage Hospital, Northallerton. Above: Manufacturing equipment for a client in the food industry. Below: A Biomass Boiler installed at Guisbrough Hall.

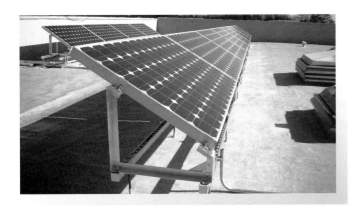

The department is registered with the Electrical Contractors Association (ECA) the Electric Council (NICEIC), and all employees are JIB graded.

The electical department went from strength to strength with contacts undertaken for various clients with the first medium size project with The Shaw Trust new office development in Middlesbrough.

Other work quickly followed: HMYOI Wetherby required new electrical infrastructure and refurbishments works including 11Kv High voltage installation and standby generator installation, Sunderland Royal Hospital received energy centre and infrastructure upgrades, at Bede College Billingham work consisted of a new build college and sports facility and for Glaxo Smith Kline GRL assisted with the insallation of new labs and a test facility. Various small works and maintenance contracts with universities, colleges and charitable trusts have also been numerous.

GRL's electrical department is also involved with renewable energy installations and energy saving installations to various NHS trusts and police departments. They included the installation of photovoltaic panels and low energy lighting and control installations.

Company founder Geoffrey Robinson is very involved with his trade association, which for the first 104 years was known as the Heating and Ventilating Contractors' Association. In 2012 it was renamed the Building & Engineering Services Association. In 2005 Geoffrey was proud to be appointed the Association's National President. Today, with businesses needing to embrace renewable energy and carbon reduction, GRL is providing Biomass heating, Biomass CHP, Solar PV and Solar Thermal installations for the industrial, public an commercial sectors. Additionally, Energy Saving solutions, Ground Source and Air Source Heat Pumps are also part of the services offered.

Geoffrey Robinson Limited is ready to be of service supplying, installing, operating and maintaining boilers and environmental building services. The firm also offers in-house mechanical, electrical, ductwork, insulation and maintenance.

The company has grown through its reputation and the development of close-working relationships with clients within both the public and private sectors.

From its inception Geoffrey Robinson Limited has undergone many changes but it still has the same values as it did when it was founded in 1971: honesty, loyalty, value for money, excellent customer service and exceptional standards.

Top left: One of Geoffrey Robinson's solar PV installations. *Left:* Geoffrey Robinson giving his inaugural speech as President of the Heating and Ventilating Contractors' Association in 2005. *Below:* Geoffrey Robinson Ltd's premises on Cowpen Industrial Estate.

William Lane
The Last of the Many

The firm was founded in 1862 by three Lanes who all lived on Smith Street, Stockton: William Lane described as a 'Brass finisher', John Lane a 'Brass Moulder' and James Lane a 'Blacksmith'. The original foundry was located on Middle Street, Stockton.

In 1907, the business relocated to its current site on Forty Foot Road. The original buildings were timber-framed with three coke-fired furnaces built into the floor. In those days there were no cranes, everything was lifted by hand. The new site was in the heartland of the iron and steel-making district of north Middlesbrough, and many of those nearby businesses were everyday customers for what was described as a 'breakdown and jobbing foundry'.

It's hard to believe now, but at one time there were up to 140 businesses in the Middlesbrough district described as 'Foundries'. William Lane Ltd, based in Forty Foot Road, is the only one still operating.

In 2012 William Lane's celebrated its 150th year of making quality sand castings on Teesside.

Making the effort to fully understand the machining requirements of customers' components is a critical investment for William Lane Ltd. Castings are made using certified ingots from Quality Assured Suppliers; the company doesn't mix in unidentifiable scrap that could compromise the integrity of its castings and affect their machinability.

A new foundry building was constructed on the site in 1939. The original foundry is now used as a store for patterns. The new building was of brick and had seven coke furnaces built into the floor which were still used (though only occasionally) until 2000.

The company remained in the Lane family until 1976, when it was sold to neighbouring steel business, Parson & Crosland Ltd - although a descendant of the firm's founders, Roy Lane, stayed with the company until 1984.

Top left: Staff outside the Machine Shop in 1958. **Bottom left:** *Casting in the Foundry in 1970's.* **Centre:** *A plaque commemorating William Lane Ltd's 150 years in business.* **Below:** *William Lane's Forty Foot Road premises, home to the company since 1907.*

Many people involve themselves in restoration projects, and the company has made replacement parts for water mills, traction engines, vintage cars, tractors and motor cycles - and even cannons. Components for the rebuild of Puffing Billy and the Steam Elephant at Beamish were produced in the foundry, as well as repair-work on the Flying Scotsman at the National Railway Museum, York, and also a number of parts for the recently completed Tornado in Darlington.

The firm is also able to manufacture highly personalised items such as commemorative plaques and benches, as well as much larger castings. William Lane works with a number of large companies that service industrial sectors such as steel (making & rolling), petrochemical, power generation and marine to produce complex castings with intricate cores to meet their specialist needs.

John Webb was appointed General Manager of the company when it was taken over, and in the same year took on Stuart Duffy and Dave Stuart as 15-year-old apprentices. Stuart is now a Director and shareholder, and remains ably supported by Dave.

At the end of 2007, parent company Parson & Crosland Ltd was sold; however, the shareholders retained William Lane Ltd which became a standalone company once more. Edward Bilcliffe now works in the Company as its MD, and is the majority shareholder.

Whilst many volume foundries have struggled to cope with competition from emerging economies such as China and gone out of business, William Lane Ltd has stuck to its original niche of providing bespoke castings on a short lead-time basis in any quantity from one upwards. Fundamentally, the foundry's products remain 'hand-made' by its highly-experienced staff, who work closely with customers to solve their engineering problems.

The foundry can remake broken or worn out metal items from the original piece. Anyone repairing old wrought ironwork, renewing old cast iron guttering, or needing a replacement grate for a fireplace can get help from William Lane. The firm also makes finials, intricate and decorative posts, staircase spindles, railing panels and posts, guttering and fixings. In fact most old castings can be reproduced faithfully to the original.

The company offers a quick and reliable lead time, and never makes promises it knows it can't keep. This is encapsulated in the firm's Mission statement: 'To develop and sustain Middlesbrough's Foundry Heritage, providing a flexible and intimate service that solves our customers' engineering problems'.

Top left: At work inside the William Lane foundry. *Above:* Making a mould for castings. The process involves mixing silica sand with sodium silicate and hardening off with carbon dioxide. *Left:* Managing Director Edward Bilcliffe. *Below:* The William Lane team pictured at the unveiling of the commemorative plaque in October 2012.

C.L. Prosser - Waste Not Want Not

C.L. Prosser & Company Limited based at Normanby Wharf, Dockside Road, Middlesbrough, specialises in ferrous and non-ferrous metals. They offer demolition, industrial dismantling and factory and site clearance services together with waste management solutions and a comprehensive skip hire service that allows its clients to control their waste disposal with an environmentally sustainable and cost effective solution to all waste disposal requirements.

The firm's Dockside Road site even has a specialist wharf facility which can be used as an off and on loading site for most materials, some of which are exported worldwide; an on-site weighbridge will record any road transported loads which are either delivered, or leave, by way of the public highway.

Prosser's story began in 1941 when the well known company of L Bainbridge & Sons was established by Leslie and Selina (Lena) Bainbridge.

Leslie was one of seven children and had served his time as a butcher, working in his father's shop until, after being left an orphan at the age of fourteen, the family sold the shop. He spent the next few years exploring all kinds of avenues to make ends meet before he and his wife found premises in Portrack Lane, known as The Villas and began a business dismantling vehicles for spare parts and selling the residue for scrap.

Top left: Miss Wallace, T R. Bainbridge's auntie, Mr Timothy Ruecroft Bainbridge and their apprentice outside the shop in 1897. *Below left:* Family members at the opening of Norton Motors in 1967, from left to right: Mrs Lena Bainbridge, Mr J. W. Mason, Cyril Bainbridge, Mr and Mrs R. Wilson. *Bottom left:* Another picture from the opening of Norton Motors in 1967 with, back row: Theresa Bainbridge, Ernie Moonie, Maureen Bainbridge, Cyril Bainbridge, Harry Dowling, Leslie Bainbridge Sr, John W Mason, Leslie Bainbridge Jr and two colleagues. Front row: Tim Bainbridge, Robert Lawson, Mary Dowling and Alan Cash. *Above:* Villa Car Sales in the late 1960s. *Below:* A family outing in 1962 with a young Robert holding Grandma Lena's hand and Dorothy Bainbridge with the white handbag.

As the effects of the war receded, the family could spend more time concentrating on the business. The children, Cyril and Leslie Junior, became more involved in the day-to-day running of the firm. Leslie, Lena and Leslie Junior took care of the car sales whilst Cyril expanded the auto spares section, which led to the acquisition of C.L. Prosser & Co. Ltd in 1953.

In the early years of C.L. Prosser there was hardly any machinery used, most activities were carried out manually; but as time progressed and the business grew materials were processed by mechanical 'alligator' shears and transported to steel works by railway.

L. Bainbridge and Sons Ltd. remained at Portrack Lane until 1976, whilst building a further garage and car sale showroom in 1967 known as Norton Motors, on Norton Road, Stockton. Both the garages were sold in the late 1970s and C.L. Prosser & Co. Ltd was expanded, leading to the purchase of a depot at South Bank, Middlesbrough, allowing the company to provide a service in the metals recycling industry throughout the North East.

Today, C.L. Prosser supplies ferrous and non-ferrous metals to steelworks and foundries throughout the United Kingdom and has obtained outlets for material for export world wide. Customers range from householders to major national companies. The company has expanded into demolition and industrial dismantling and running a comprehensive waste and skip hire service.

Recycling is the way of the future, and with this in mind C.L. Prosser now provides recyclable materials which are then processed into useable raw materials.

Four generations of the Bainbridge family have now been involved with the company. The youngest members think back with pride on their parents', grandparents' and great grandparents' efforts, sharing a determination to succeed and appreciating the hard work of those who did the groundwork which helped build the business into what it is today.

C.L. Prosser is run today by Cyril and his family: Ronnie, Robert and Lena.

The firm's founding traditions continue, and whilst the company contributes to the metals recycling industry, it also provides employment to some 40 people whilst it endeavours to maintain a steady expansion, growing on the strength of its reputation.

Top left: *The yard of C.L. Prosser & Co at South Bank, Middlesbrough in 1969.* **Below left:** *A C.L Prosser vehicle with cargo of industrial machinery waiting to be off-loaded and dismantled.* **Centre:** *The Directors of C.L. Prosser in 1999, from left to right: Ronnie Bainbridge, Lena Bainbridge Jr, Cyril Bainbridge and Robert Bainbridge.* **Top right:** *C.L. Prosser's wharf for ship loading and export of materials world wide.* **Below:** *A bird's eye view of Normanby Wharf.*

Suggitt's Quality Ices

Is there anything that evokes memories of warm summer days more than ice cream? And if ordinary ice cream can do the trick then the very best ice cream does it even better.

A Suggitt Ltd, the ice cream makers based at 93, High Street, Great Ayton, have been tickling our taste buds since the 1920s. But if it's a hot day get there early if you want to enjoy one of the firm's delicious ice cream cornets – the long queues for Suggitt's famous quality ices on a summer's day tell their own tale.

The business began when Arthur Suggitt and his wife Bertha opened a confectionery shop at 14-15 High Green where Mrs Suggitt began making ice cream at the weekends.

Back in those days there were no fridges or freezers. Blocks of ice were collected from the docks, crushed and added to brine to reduce the temperature still further. The salted ice could be used to freeze ice cream and to cool storage freezers. Though in later years dried milk powder would be used in the Suggitt's special recipe, in those early days fresh milk had to be simmered overnight to evaporate some of the water, creating a thicker liquid for use in the ice cream making process

Alan Suggitt, the person who would eventually take the business to new heights of success, was born in 1922. His childhood was for other boys an enviable one, one in which ice cream was a constant presence. In 1939 however, the outbreak of the Second World War would see ice cream production halted due to the shortage of ice. It was not until 1945 that production began again. Ice cream production moved from behind the confectionery shop to new premises next to Greenbank in 1956.

Top left: Alan Suggitt. **Above and below:** *Two views of Suggitt's 1950s trailer on the Stokesley to Helmsley Road. In the bottom picture Alan is at the counter, his sister Margorie and father Arthur (Artie) are standing beside the car.*

By the mid-1970s, everyone who visited Great Ayton was dropping in at Suggitt's increasingly famous sweetshop and café for a cup of coffee or tea, or better still a wafer or cornet of Suggitt's distinctive ice cream. According to Alan Suggitt, who had seen the premises double in size, "it's more like a club for local people than a café because it's quiet and pleasant. We don't have anything like juke boxes to shatter the peace."

Alan and Joyce's son, Peter, worked with his parents in the business until 1975 when he joined the Royal Air Force. As a result the firm's second ice cream van was no longer used. Peter Suggitt, who now runs the business, returned from the RAF to rejoin the family firm in 1987.

Five years later in 1961, the shop was extended into the former house next door and the original shop was turned over to storage.

As soon as he was old enough, Alan Suggitt would ride to local beauty spots with his motorcycle and sidecar, the sidecar loaded with ice cream. The motorcycle would eventually give way to a van with weekend routes around Great Ayton and Stokesley giving way to a regular spot on the Plane at Stokesley and later at West Green. A second van was bought to go around local farms and villages as well as local village shows in such places as Castleton, Danby and Killdale.

Alan's mother, Bertha, a native of Stockton, who had moved to Great Ayton after leaving school, died in 1964. She would be remembered by thousands of people who had been served by her with ice cream on their visits to the village. Following her death, the limited company A Suggitt Ltd was formed.

SUGGITT'S...
Quality Ices
93 High Street
GREAT AYTON

Change came in 1971 when fire caused by a fault in newly-installed wiring damaged the old shop. It was demolished and a café added to the business.

Alan Suggitt and his wife Joyce now ran the café, ice cream making operation and two ice cream vans. Both Alan and Joyce dispensed ice cream from their vans in and around Stokesley for many years.

The last ice cream van was disposed of in 1988 at the same time as Joyce Suggitt retired. Alan Suggit died in 2001; sadly, Joyce followed him in 2002.

Today, Peter Suggitt continues the fine family tradition begun by his grandmother Bertha in the 1920s. Her winning recipe ensures that serious ice cream aficionados still to flock to Great Ayton to experience ice cream, just like it used to taste.

Top left: *Alan Suggitt pictured alongside one of the company's ice cream vans.* **Left:** *A familiar sight to the people of Teesside, this image has been in use on Suggitt bags since the 1950s.* **Below:** *Peter Suggitt, 2012.*

Teesside University - Inspiring Progress

Teesside University has been serving local needs since the early 20th century. The origins of the University lie in the generosity of local shipping magnate, Joseph Constantine. Between 1916 and the opening of the college named after him by the then Prince of Wales in 1930, Constantine donated over £80,000 to the enterprise.

The College grew steadily, with about 2,000 students by the outbreak of the Second World War.

During the war, Constantine College provided training and educational services to the essential war industries. One vital function was technical training for the many women who replaced men conscripted into the forces. The College also engaged in the production of specialist equipment.

Post-war the College struggled to accommodate rising demand, especially the growth of day release of young workers. The number of full-time students also increased. At the same time the number of students on externally validated degree courses expanded.

During the 1960s, the orientation of the College was broadened to include Liberal Studies. Meanwhile, the old High School buildings were acquired and the highly visible eleven-storey tower block was built.

In 1970, Constantine College became Teesside Polytechnic. Middlesbrough became a university town in 1992 when the polytechnic became a university. Since then the campus has changed dramatically with new halls of residence, an award-winning Library and two new School of Health and Social Care buildings. Other developments have been the Phoenix and Athena buildings, where students can study at the cutting edge of digital technology.

Over 9,000 students are now enrolled on health and social care courses. Students can also study computer games design, physiotherapy, sport and exercise, media studies, forensic science, law, graphic design, travel and tourism or local modern and medieval history. The University also offers programmes in fine art and the performing arts, as well as business studies.

The founders of Constantine College would be delighted that their creation was the 2009 University of the Year and has become an institution with over 2,000 staff and of almost 30,000 students, meeting the educational and workforce development needs of the 21st century.

Top: Joseph Constantine. **Left:** *The original Constantine Building in 1930.* **Below:** *Teesside University Library Building, 2013.*

Harrison Packaging

THIS STONE WAS LAID BY THE MAYOR OF STOCKTON ALD. JOHN HARRISON, ESQ. J.P. OCTOBER 3RD 1907

Harrison Packaging, based at Teesside Industrial Estate, Thornaby, is one of the oldest independent printed carton manufacturers in Europe and privately owned companies on Teesside. Operating from modern, purpose-built premises covering over 70,000 sq. ft., it provides environmentally sustainable packaging solutions to the Healthcare, Food and Household markets.

A continuous investment and improvement programme has ensured that the company has 'state of the art', efficient equipment embracing the very latest technology, with the ability to print up to seven colours along with a variety of coatings in one pass. The business can achieve the most challenging of designs on a variety of different materials.

Customers include not only large 'Blue Chip' brand owners but, also numerous specialist producers. Harrison's support for customers, whatever their size, has helped many niche companies grow, particularly in the early stages of their development.

The business established in 1882, became a limited company in 1910. John Harrison (Stockton) Limited was started as a general print company by John Harrison, who went on to become Mayor of Stockton on five occasions. Reputedly won on a game of cards, the business remained in the ownership of the Harrison family until a management buyout in 2003. Chairman Sir Colin Harrison retired in 2006 after 40 years' service and the present directors retain ownership.

At first based on Norton Road, Stockton, the business moved to Portrack Lane in 1950 becoming a major supplier of printing, leaflets and rigid boxes. With the acquisition of Heavisides, another local company, healthcare leaflet production was expanded.

Today, Harrison Packaging focuses entirely on printed cartons for the Food, Healthcare and Houseware markets. It is one of only a handful of companies in Europe approved to manufacture both food and pharmaceutical products on a single site. Now with 120 employees, investment and organic growth has transformed the business into one of the UK's leading carton producers.

Meanwhile, many historical items connected with John Harrison (Stockton) Limited and Heavisides Limited from the past 130 years can be found at Preston Farm Museum.

The business has been built on producing quality products, delivered on time, with excellent customer service from committed employees. The present directors very much intend that the business continues to match those high standards for many years to come.

Top left: A photograph from 1907 with John Harrison in the foreground in his position as Mayor of Stockton. *Below:* Harrison's Teesside Industrial Estate, Thornaby, premises.

ACKNOWLEDGMENTS

The publishers would like to sincerely thank the following individuals and organisations for their help and contribution to this publication.

Middlesbrough Reference Library

Getty Images

Mirrorpix

Stan Laundon, Jim Sculley and Eric Whitehouse
for supplying the local band photographs

We would also like to thank Andy from Wood's Library's Flickr photostream for supplying the majority of transport pictures in this book. He has kindly allowed us to use a selection of images, mainly buses, from his extensive collection taken mainly in the 60s and 70s. Some older readers may remember Wood's shop at the top end of High Street, in Stockton, which became known as 'Wood's Corner'.

Andy's paternal great grandfather was a Londoner who was appointed to open the branch of W H Smith on the station at Stockton-on-Tees in the 19th century. He later went on to open his own shop selling books, stationery and toys on Stockton High Street. His grandfather took over this business after World War One, and in the mid-1930s, sold it and bought a new shop at 111 Lanehouse Road in nearby Thornaby, selling similar merchandise and running a lending library. He sold the shop on retirement in the early 1950s. The photograph shows Wood's Library around 1948.